Creative Colloquy
VOLUME ONE

Edited by Joshua Swainston   Forward by Jackie Fender

Cover & Artwork by Michaela Eaves

Creative Colloquy
Tacoma, WA
www.CreativeColloquy.com

ISBN-13: 978-0692296479

ISBN-10: 0692296476

This book is dedicated to the scholars and scribes,

the lovers of the written word,

and the enthusiasts of the creative community.

Creative (kree-ey-tiv) -adjective: having the quality or power of creating resulting from originality of thought, expression, etc.

+

Colloquy (kol-uh-kwee) –noun: a conversational exchange; dialogue, a conference.

=

Creative Colloquy -community: literary site and review AKA word nerds and storytellers gathering upon pages, cyberspace and in person to share their prose.

Dear Readers,

Creative Colloquy began as a submission based literary site focusing on Tacoma and South Sound scribes, while paying special attention to short stories, essays and excerpts of larger pieces. Since February of 2014, we have been investing into our literary community. Creative Colloquy was born from the desire to create a platform for writers to share their work and build relationships with those of like minds.

A distinct aspect of Creative Colloquy's vision has always been to foster relationships through the mutual admiration of the written word. We do this in a number of ways by abandoning our keyboards to connect with the community and coordinating events. While striving to bridge gaps between genres and generations we have had the divine opportunity of discovering immense talent and have read phenomenal stories. Stories that are begging to be read from paper pages. So here we are, Creative Colloquy Volume One.

While I make mention of the local talent, let me clarify, this is not a book about Tacoma, nor is it a book about the South Sound, but the product of artist who happen to live in the region. Our creative culture is a deep well in Tacoma (and Olympia and everywhere in-between) thanks to both Tacoma natives and transplants from all over the globe. It's our mission to do due diligence to encourage the bonds built in the literary community. This collection before you is just a beginning.

Creative Colloquy Volume One includes literary fictions, non-fictional essays and poetic prose, all exquisite displays of storytelling, transporting readers through the crafting of words. We hope to contribute to both the oral and written tradition of storytelling and our own local creative community by sharing these stories before you.

We have received an immense level of community support in our efforts and are honored to have the opportunity to present to you this collection. The authors within are teachers, parents, students, 9to5ers—an eclectic and diverse example of what it means to be a writer. This is to say, it takes all types to concoct the myriad of lush scenery and layered personality throughout these pages. The Creative Colloquy team only hopes to bring these stories to reading eyes and ready minds, to foster our literary community by investing ourselves and our passion to realize this vision.

"The unread story is not a story; it is little black marks on wood pulp. The reader, reading it, makes it live: a live thing, a story."

\- Ursula K. Le Guin

This book exists so that you, the reader, can breathe lives into these stories by narrating them with your imaginations.

Thank you and enjoy.

~Jackie Fender

Founder

In the month of August, 2014, Creative Colloquy ran an Indiegogo campaign to fund this book. These wonderful people contributed.

- Ron Swarner
- Marguerite Giguere
- L Susan Jasica
- William Kupinse
- Megan Barney
- Nyle Swainston
- Billie Grace
- Kim Thompson
- Craig Arlen Rounds
- Jenson Charnell
- Jon Elston
- The Nearsighted Narwhal
- Michelle Nikisch
- Laura Phipps
- Tiffany Price
- The Rejected Writer
- 9 Lives Studios
- Lory French
- Karen Harris Tully
- Stacy Ellis
- Laurel Cay

From the team at Creative Colloquy, thank you.

Table of Content

Squirrels Hate Robots

William Turbyfill

"Squirrels hate robots." He says it with such earnestness that it catches me off guard.

"I beg your pardon."

"Squirrels. Hate. Robots. It's really not that complicated." The five year old is right. It is not a complicated concept to comprehend and yet, I have questions, not the least of which is, 'if squirrels hate robots, do robots in turn, hate squirrels?' "I could draw you a picture of it if that would make it easier for you." I'm not a fan of his condescending attitude.

"How do you know this, about the robots and the squirrels and what not?" I say this while looking for a pencil and paper. As much as I want to smack him, if I'm honest, I also really want him to draw me a picture of squirrels hating on robots.

"Everyone knows that." Do they? Is that another one of those bits of information that everyone knows but that I somehow missed out on? Like how mortgages work or how a person goes about scheduling dentist appointments. I'm well past the age where I can be given a free pass on things like that. Is the instinctual animosity that all squirrels have towards robots the newest thing?

"Of course, I mean. I know that and you know that I know that," I pause waiting for him to acknowledge that he knows that I know that. He looks up from his blocks, gives me an impatient nod and I continue. "But what do you think about that?"

"What do I think about what?"

"Do you think it's fair, I mean right? What's your position on the whole squirrel robot thing?"

"Well," the cherub's chubby little fingers put down the blocks and he crosses his arms in a look of deep contemplation. "That's a big question. You have to look at it from both sides. Robots are not born like squirrels are, they are made by people. And squirrels are not made by people; they are born from other squirrels." There is nothing in that that I can argue with. "Now squirrels live in trees and what are trees made of?"

I hadn't realized that I was going to be asked questions. Before I can think of an intelligent answer, I shout out, "Bark!"

He looks at me like I'm an eye chart.

"No. Wood. Trees are made of wood. The bark is just decoration. Now, where do robots live?"

Shit. Where do robots live? I mean, do robots even live? Is this a trick question? Is this little pip squeak trying to make a fool out of me on some sort of technicality? Okay, let's think this through. Robots are inorganic life that rely on Artificial Intelligence that stems ultimately from human programming and construction; no actually, they got robots that build robots now. Mental note to remind this kid later that not all robots are made by people like he said they were. Oh no, he's staring. Think of something quick; just don't say 'bark'.

"Um... not trees."

"Exactly!" Nailed it. "Robots live everywhere but trees. They are in houses, underwater, airplanes and outer space. The only place Robots don't live is in trees."

"With the squirrels." I say showing that I'm tracking him.

"With the squirrels," he responds before going back to playing with his blocks thus inaugurating the longest silence I have ever experienced in my life. Is that it? Does that explain everything? What the hell does that have to do with anything? Am I having a stroke? Why would a tree dwelling rat give two shits about robots? Unless...do they feel threatened? Are squirrels aware of the encroachment of robotic life into all ecosystems both natural and man-made with trees being the last bastion of robot-less freedom? And why haven't they been able to encroach into trees yet? Oh my god, are the squirrels fending them off somehow? Are they aware on some deep rooted level of consciousness that the advent of the singularity is at hand and with its fulfillment all life on earth will suffer and be subjugated under the titanium fist of emotionless robotic rule? Are the squirrels protecting us from total annihilation? I mean on some level it makes sense of course, robots are cold and calculating but squirrels, well, whether one believes in God or evolution, both humans and squirrels come from the same life source, the same heartbeat that gave birth to humanity also birth

forth the noble squirrel. They are our earthborn brethren and allies against the factory-made menace. How many squirrels have given their lives in an attempt to free us from our dependence on the automobile? Sure, their approach is flawed in its execution, but their intention and motive is as pure as freshly fallen snow. Never again will I pass by a squirrel killed on the street without mourning my distant kin. We are in this together little friend and together we will prevail.

The boy interrupts my thoughts, "Can I help you?"

I wipe the tears of revelation from my face and try to find the words. "I was just wondering where, I mean when it was that… I mean, fucking robots, am I right?"

"Ugh, you're such a squirrel."

The Faithful Wife

Lory French

"I told you I wasn't ever going to go into sordid details," Olivia sighed, tired of the drawn out conversation. Dave could be such a little bitch when he wanted to be. She was tired and knew that tomorrow morning was only going to bring a long march of more whining from the kids she'd be chaperoning up to Everett for a field trip on some whale watching boat. She ran her hand longingly over her empty pillow.

"I need to know now. I know I said I was ok with it, but I just …. I can't take looking at every guy we know and wondering 'Is it him? Did he know I gave permission? Is he laugh…"

"PERMISSION???" She exploded. "Permission? I for damned sure didn't need your fucking permission."

Dave threw up his hands in surrender. "That was a poor choice of words."

"Yes, the hell it was!"

"I just…..Olivia I can't take it anymore. I know what we agreed to do, and I have been trying to just let it go, but you know everything about her. Everything. What we did, where we went, how long it went on." Olivia buried her ears in her hands, willing him to shut up. "Don't do that, babe. I just need a name. I can't handle second guessing all our friends. It's making it worse."

"Making what worse?" Olivia questioned. "You. Cheated. On. Me. This is not something I brought down on us. You cheated on me. As for my 'revenge fuck,' as you wanted to call it, I can promise you it's no one you know. That's a guarantee.

Dave ripped off the covers and paced at the foot of the bed. "You can't know that. You can't know that."

Olivia watched Dave as he fretted at the other side of the room, raking his fingers through his graying hair. The motion caused his well-defined torso to ripple in a way she might otherwise have appreciated. "What's setting this off, Dave?"

Something in her tone caused him to stand still, hands by his side, and stare at her. "What do you mean?" he said.

"It's been seven years," she continued in her measured tones. "Seven years since all this went down, and I thought we were finally past it. I don't wake up in a panic anymore, imagining you left me for her." He protested with a sigh and a raised finger, as if he had a point to make, then went back to pacing. "I finally stopped going through your texts. I don't freak out when you're a little bit late, or if you have a 'meeting go late,'" she made air quotes.

"I'm not cheating, if that's what you mean. I'm not!" He slumped into the armchair, idly stroking the upholstery. "I'm really not, Olivia. There hasn't been anyone else. I mean, you know, not since then." Dave looked her straight in the eyes. Olivia flashed back to her friend, the Dave before the tedium of stalled careers and marital spats over who did the dishes or forgot to lock the doors, the Dave before he trashed her heart all over their living room with the power of one phone call.

"OK," she said. "I believe you. But it's really still none of your business. Those were the terms."

"Please, O," he pleaded quietly, "Please. I didn't know it would feel like this. I just wanted to say anything to make you stay. I was making a deal I thought would make it all right. I didn't know it would eat at me for the rest of my goddamned life."

Olivia rolled her eyes and massaged the back of her neck. "Isn't that the point, Dave?   I didn't agree to this to make you feel GOOD about yourself. It wasn't a picnic for me finding out you'd betrayed me while I was pregnant with Shane. Finding out because the bitch called me to cry you'd left her. And this was you, your idea, telling me to go fuck someone. You had that goddamned affair. You brought someone into our marriage while I was pregnant with our son and then told ME to go do the same thing to make it BETTER? And now you're surprised that it's not working for YOU? I'm tired. I have an ass-long day tomorrow and I am really actually getting sick of being tired. Sleep on the couch if you want to. I'm done with this for tonight."

She clicked off the light and left him to find his way in the dark while she curled up on her side, facing the edge of the bed. He fumbled his way across the room, stubbing his toe just the disappointing once. She scowled in the dark as he made his way under the covers, wrapping his arm around her soft middle, cupping the breast nearest the mattress in his way that usually made her feel belonging. Tonight it felt like possession. She shrugged and he released her breast, but kept her waist encircled.

"O," Dave murmured into her neck. "I know I don't deserve you. But I love you. I do. I love the family we've made. I hate that I fucked it up. But can't you forgive me?"

"Clearly I forgave you, you're in my bed," said Olivia. "Shut up and go to sleep."

Dave curled his free hand in her hair, resting it on the pillow above her head. "If you forgive me, then we shouldn't have secrets between us. Not even this." Olivia stiffened as he changed tack. Sensing a soft spot, he rolled on. "I agree with you babe, I really don't want to know any details. I just need to clear the air, to keep from wanting to fucking punch every man who ever talks to you."

Olivia turned her sudden grin to the pillow, trying not to laugh at the absurdity of the image of boxing gym Dave decking an unsuspecting farmer right over the produce stall at the farmer's market.

"Dammit, Dave."

"Please," he whispered. "Just a name. Then I will drop it. Forever."

"Do you promise?" She demanded. "Forever? Done? I'm so sick of this and I want it gone from our lives."

"Gone. Over. Done." He squeezed her in affirmation.

She could feel his tension and her own bone-deep fatigue. What the hell. "No one." The palpable silence raised the volume of her heart to a drumbeat.

"That's not cute, Olivia." His tone was clearly annoyed.

"It's not meant to be. No one. I never did it. I had a 6 month old baby and I wasn't about to go spill breast milk all over some random guy to make you feel better about your guilt. Maybe you didn't care who touched me, but I sure as hell did. I wouldn't have felt clean coming back to Shane like that. And fuck it, I was too goddamned tired for that shit." She closed her eyes, her long secret finally out.

Dave ripped himself away from her. He stumbled into the nightstand as he propelled himself out of the bed. "You bitch!" He snapped on his light, "You fucking bitch!"

"WHAT?" Wide awake now, Olivia sat upright and turned to face her seething husband. "You should be glad I didn't give it up to someone. You should realize the value of what I am saying to you. And no more wanting to box the neighbors, yeah?"

"This isn't funny!" he shouted, stabbing a finger in her direction. "You lied to me. You let me believe we were even, that it was ok. Seven years of this shit, of me wondering, you-- you lying!"

Olivia watched him in growing hollow sadness. "For real, Dave?" she said as tears starting to form, tears she vowed not to let fall. "You're worried about being even? You found out you have a faithful wife and you're pissed about that?"

"About being tricked? Incensed," he affirmed with a grunt, snatching his pillow and the blanket folded at the foot of the bed. "I'm sleeping on the couch, you troll." Dave stalked out of the room, leaving his light on, the door open, and a trail of indignation behind him.

Olivia ignored the door, reached over the bed to switch off Dave's light, and then curled back into her usual position. Despite the vague ache in her heart, sleep came surely for her. Dave, he could suck it.

Silver

Christian Carvajal

In those days, the year of our Lord Jesus Christ one thousand seven hundred and eighty-seven, Paris was a city abuzz with death. It buzzed as a topic of conversation: in the private apartments of His Majesty King Louis XVI at Versailles; in the salons of nobles (who fretted, too, about the aroma of revolution in the air); and in taverns, soon to be called bistrots, in which lesser men shouted and sang around mouthfuls of veal. It buzzed in the clouds of pernicious insects thickening the air over churchyard cemeteries. And it buzzed in the streets, as soldiers, executioners, and laborers made use of what few livres they earned, some by killing, others by handling the remains.

For it was in that year that millions of erstwhile Parisians, some nestled safely in the arms of their Father above, some wailing and roasting beneath our feet, saw their mortal remains transported from the overflowing Cemetery of the Holy Innocents and many other places into quarries nearby. These tunnels, first mined by our Roman forebears, were to be employed as an Empire of the Dead, an ossuary that stretched on for leagues. Thus, the noxious smells and gruesome remains of our ancestors from centuries past were to be relocated between earth and Hell. I, like many others who lived in the shadow of Montparnasse, had been hired by the Council of State to assist in the exhumation and transportation of bodies. It was grim, malodorous, pestilent work, the kind that draws men together even as it enflames their weary spines. Yet I suppose even the most burdensome labor may grow routine after a time; and so it was that I struck up a friendship with a fellow I was proud to call Henri. A large man, broad-shouldered and strong as a wall, he seemed to have been made for such work. Never once did I observe him so much as scowling or flinching, though the spectacles of Hades affronted us daily.

Henri and I would load an empty horse cart with a tangle of sickening remains in the cemetery, cover this soulless matter with black cloth, and then drive the cart south through the Barrière d'Enfer, or Hell Gate. A resigned priest marched beside us, singing prayers to the best of his ability the entire way. Upon its arrival, the cart would sit until nightfall, at which time a priest would speak another series of prayers, then step away so we could carry our ghastly freight down into the quarry by torchlight. I never thought to question why so many fervently uttered prayers were directed at matter which had already relinquished its appointed souls, nor why such rites occurred in the dead of night. It was simply the way these things were done.

Would that I had been more curious, though surely such as I could never have anticipated the unholy events which befell late that summer. It was unseasonably cool that evening, and the sun had just descended on its heavenly course below the western horizon. We had driven our first of the night's cartloads through the Hell Gate and up to the mouth of the tunnel. We unyoked the horses; a boy led them away to be watered. The priest completed his praying and, upon his "amen," backed away so we could untie and pull away the cloth. I wadded the inky raiment and set it aside for a subsequent load.

In such circumstances, of course, it would not have been greatly surprising had the contents of the cart assailed our nostrils, though the wagon loads often smelled like nothing more offensive than earth. Yet the first hint of trouble was a cloying miasma of sweetness. I have since been told this smell may accompany disease, as of those festering maladies encountered in equatorial lands. All I knew at the time was astonishment. Henri startled to attention. "Foul monster!" he cried, and then, Titan that he was, he lost no time in backing away from the cart. Distracted by this movement, I did not see the pile of bodies shift beside me until it was too late to remove myself from any danger. What happened next, may Almighty God see fit to at long last remove from my dreams.

At first it seemed a skeleton, dressed still in clods and ribbons of flesh, was prying itself loose from between the other bodies. I stared, goggle-eyed, as it exposed first its skull, then its jutting shoulder bone, then an arm, the bony fingers of which scrabbled toward me and clutched at my own person. I confess to have lost whatever powers of reason I may normally possess. You will think, perhaps, no less of me if I made water which spread down my legs. In all those long months of carrying the dead, never once had I imagined such horrors. Until that moment, the common dead had been sufficient food for my nightmares, yet now I saw the skeleton moving itself; nay, in truth rotting flesh manipulated the gnarled bones from within like a puppet in a marketplace spectacle. As its claw pulled me closer, I saw, by the flickering glow of the torches, that what I had first taken to be human carrion was even fouler than that. A fetid rope composed of something very like worms filled the marrow, congealed into a muscular tangle that writhed like a serpent of once-human flesh. A beast was coiled inside that skeleton, inhabiting and articulating it as a crab fills its shell. The eyes of something horrid, I must even say demonic, stared wildly from the ocular recesses of the skull. Whatever it was, I sensed innately that its long hibernation or entrapment underground had driven it steadily and irrevocably mad.

I was unaware in that moment that mighty Henri had grabbed me by my collar and was tugging as hard as he could, hard enough to lengthen its threads near to snapping. Yet even his enormous strength was no match for the beast, which strained against moldy bones hard enough to crack them lengthwise. "A torch," Henri exclaimed. "Give it to me—now!" A young priest nearby, emboldened, no doubt, by his vigorous faith in the succors of Heaven, withdrew a torch from its sconce and approached Henri's side. In the mere instant my brave companion needed to grab and gain control of that torch, the snapping serpent-flesh within the moldering skull shot forward. Like a spear tip, its snout jabbed into the crook of my elbow. A jet of scarlet betrayed the great thirst of the monster, which I now saw was probing for blood in the deepest meats and sinews of my arm.

Henri had seized the torch, and now thrust it into the demon's encapsulating skull. Upon contact, the fire made a great hissing noise against the ungodly meat of the creature. The foul thing then retracted its stinger of a maw, which exuded clots of thick, mucous ichor at its tip. The sharpened proboscis danced about wildly, whether seeking new prey or performing Saint Vitus' dance I cannot say. My arm, infected with satanic foulness, hurt as though it had been branded. This agony now spread toward my shoulder as the claws of the demon finally surrendered their grip on my vestments. Reduced to the infantile crawl of a sot, I gibbered in utmost terror as I fell on my back and wriggled away from the fire-maddened hydra. My wound left a trail in the earth like the filth of a slug.

Recovering its wits, the serpent turned its baleful glare fully toward Henri. My friend redoubled his attack; soon others found courage enough to assist him. The beast struggled with fearful determination, yet half its skeletal apartment was still wedged between the bodies in the cart. It was therefore unable to withdraw, or to engage in further mischief by fleeing northward into the city, nor by slithering deep into the bowels of our subterranean ossuary. The flames, which illuminated the skull and ribs from within, ignited and gnawed at the devil's flesh. A loathsome evaporation of marsh gas escaped this foul lantern to hang thickly about the mouth of the quarry. Slowly, gradually, as if the beast were formed of wet pitch, its sinews were fully consumed. It relinquished its struggles, then returned at long last to the domain of demons.

The next thing I knew, Henri was hunched over me, his face pallid and damp with perspiration. "I can help you," said he, "but it will cost me dear! Ah, well, 'tis fortunate for you that I deem you worthy of the expense."

I made some response, God knows what. The pain of the venom robbed me of thoughts and was worse than I could bear. It seemed to me a vast pressure had grown inside my extremity and would soon free itself by splitting the skin in the manner of an overstuffed sausage. I uttered desperate and agonized shrieks. In my wretchedness, it felt as though my flesh had been made swollen with child. Perhaps it had, as when a spider injects its wriggling young within a wasp so that the victim becomes a womb, then a maggot's first meal. "Henri!" I cried mournfully. "Henri!"

He unlaced his purse and withdrew a small, corked phial. He set it aside, then clutched at my arm and squeezed with all his might. The gash popped like an ulcer, expelling a great quantity of malodorous phlegm over Henri's left shoulder and spraying the earth with thick vomit. He milked the wound of all the venom he could, my exhausted voice cursing him with foul imprecations the while. Then, Henri uncorked the phial and emptied its contents into the wound. The pain subsided a bit, enough for me to converse in the manner of a Christian. "The beast," I exclaimed. "Is it dead?"

"Never mind that," my savior replied. "Our churchmen have burned it alive."

"O, thanks be to God!"

"It is well you should honor God, truly, for it is only by His grace that you live."

"Indeed, I do live by His grace, and your strength, which you wield to His glory. But tell me, I beg you, what was that despicable creature?"

"We have no words for such monsters in the French tongue," replied he. "Few mortal Christians know, nor wish to believe, that such fell things remain in the earth. They are, perhaps, the offspring of Nephilim, re-birthed from the muck as God's Deluge subsided. The Romans knew them as striges, the drinkers of blood. They have long been held captive below; it is only in the course of this hideous transferal of bones that we encounter them again. Fortunately for you, my friend, a godly priest has discovered a physic which reverses the venom's putrefying effects. Had the stinger remained in your arm, no potion known to any man would have saved you, yet it seems to me that we may have applied it in time."

"This good potion," said I. "What is in it?"

"Lunar caustic," said he, "a salt the alchemists extract from an acid they pour over coins of pure silver. Now you see that your life has been costly indeed! I procured this phial for myself and my sons at considerable expense once I learned why these bodies were carried at night. Only then do such demons arise, revealing themselves to God's servants, who then put their damned bodies to the torch."

"Why was I never told of their existence?"

"Ha!" laughed he. "Would you have joined our merry procession, had you known what might await you at its ending?"

"By the love of God, no!" I replied.

"Wisely said! Yet these bodies must be moved, the scourge of striges within them destroyed for all time."

And so it was. The reburial of bodies continued for a year and a quarter. Humble laborer that I am, I returned to work as soon as I could, putting food on my family's table even as my nightmares deprived me of sleep. My arm, like my sleep, recovered but slowly. It remained marked with a cloudy black scar like the blemish of Cain, though from venom or silver I know not which.

This city, I hope, will soon forget these unholy terrors we encountered as our dead were re-interred within the wounds of the earth. As we delved through those seams, the beasts within them found our own flesh as well. The Devil's menagerie claimed fourteen lives that year. We burned our friends' bodies and pulverized their bones before strewing them deep in the ossuary, unmarked and before long forgotten by men. May God have mercy on the souls we thus set free.

Red

Melissa Thayer

The gun was clean. Loaded. Double-checked. His knife, the one he had carried always, she held a moment before strapping it to her belt. There were five who must die. Outside her blinded window, dawn was about to break over the minarets. The muezzin sing-songed beckonings to adhan.

The men who took him last night hadn't seen her. His body would not get cold before she enacted her revenge. The first was Gadi. He was a whore-lover. The second was Azzam, he had a scar across his face from his penchant for bar fights. Zero was famously addicted to opium. Marid sold carpets at the bazaar. Jibril was a gambler. Despite the call the adhan, she knew the hypocrites wouldn't be among the crowds.

She holstered the gun, wrapped her face in a red scarf, and took to the dark streets. They had no idea who they had awakened. First stop, Madame Khalidah's. She slipped in past the incensed parlor, whispering her question to the madame on the whereabouts of Gadi. The carpeted stairs hushed her steps, down the hall, third door on the left. She eased the door open. He was sleeping naked on the couch with a sweaty whore. He awoke to the pressure of the barrel against his temple.

She would never feel her lover's lips again.

Bang.

Before anyone knew what had happened, she had disappeared out the window, scaling the wall of the low building. She moved like a cat through the maze of streets and alleys to a bar. She didn't know if it was the right bar, she was moving on pure intuition. She cocked the gun. She stepped through the arched doorway. Her instincts served her well. Azzam and Jibril sat in a corner, sharing the hookah and drinking. She glided along the wall to the dark corner. She caught them both in her green-eyed gaze.

The beautiful words he whispered to her at night would fade.

Bang.

The eagerness in his eyes, holding a sense of adventure and mischief was gone.

Bang.

The two men slumped over the table. As fast as she had moved in, she left. She adjusted her scarf. The air was already starting to get warm. The light was breaking. Oranges were skidding across the sky. An opium den lay two alleys over. She crept past awakening merchants and feral cats twirling themselves around posts. The opium den was dark, smoky, and filled with the remnants of last night's orgy. Zero's face was still imprinted fresh in her mind. There he was. Eyes glazed over, red with bags under them. He looked dazed as he stared at the barrel between his eyes.

Honest moments without walls were stolen and she was caged and alone again. The movements of her lover's eyes and the occasional dimple from his smile were still.

Bang.

The den dwellers were too drugged to care that a corpse now slumped in their midst. The merchants in the bazaar began opening their tents. Marid's carpet shop was still dark, but his figure was shadowed against the breaking day. Plush carpets were being hung out on display. She walked up to the one he was standing behind as he hung it to the rope above. From behind her red scarf, she looked at him. His eyes were black. He had been the one who had slit his throat. He didn't have time to move before she did.

The children they would never have.

Slice.

His body dropped and she disappeared as the sunlight fell across the city. She returned to her lover, his body still slightly warm. She removed her scarf, resting the silk across his throat and face, and lay down beside him.

And Other Ways to Die

Nicholas Stillman

I walked into the apartment soaking, the rain railing against the living room window as if protesting my sudden disappearance. I collapsed. I was a wet rag, soaking into the fibers of the couch. My overcoat pooled on the carpet in front of me. My head pounded. I reached for wine.

As I poured into the tired glass on the coffee table, I watched Matthew in the kitchen, busy baptizing last night's dishes.

"Matthew," I said from across the room. "I am having an existential crisis." I find it best to start with drama to get attention. I always killed someone in the first chapter of my novels. I once murdered an entire family in the first sentence.

"Are you really? A crisis?" said Matthew, dunking another lasagna-encrusted soul into the holy pool. At least, that's how I liked to imagine how he did dishes. Matthew was a seminary school dropout. It was the first thing I learned about him after he responded to my "roommate wanted" ad three months ago. The second thing I learned about him was that he wanted to be a writer. Wanted, he had said, to be like me. Holding a rather high opinion of myself, and raised as I was without religion, the thought of living with a Catholic priest who admired my work was about as close to a realizing a long-dormant fantasy as I would ever get. Unfortunately, this priest was straight as an arrow and much too devout to be any fun.

"Well, it's not really a crisis," I admitted. "I was being theatrical." It's no use pretending with him. Matthew is too sharp for that. "But this has not been one of my better days."

Matthew wiped his hands, drained the sink, and perched in the overstuffed armchair across from me. "Do you want to talk about the funeral? You've barely said anything since you found out."

"It wasn't just the funeral, although that was…" I sipped the Cabernet.

"Now this was the other Matthew, right? Your boyfriend?" He asked, his eyes full of priest-ly sympathy.

"Matthew Zeigler," I confirmed. "Former lover." I saw the living-Matthew blush and I was pleased. I kicked off my shoes. "He died via cartwheel. Hilarious, really." I tried to smile, but nothing but a facial tick emerged. I was lying again and couldn't help it. I was a great liar. Lies were how I made my living up until that point. "He was drunk and it was a bet. His friends said no one past sixty can cartwheel. He was in great shape, Matthew was. And he just had to prove them all wrong." I found my mind lapsing into images of cool ceviche on a sweaty night out on the deck of a Vegas hotel room.

"It's OK if you don't want to tell me everything," he said. Matthew had an annoying way of using his blue eyes to penetrate through walls of bullshit.

"Yeah, well, stomach cancer is much too boring," I said. The wine had begun wrapping its arms around my prefrontal cortex in its toasty embrace and I studied my roommate from behind my glass: a bit on the scrawny side, with a mop of black hair and knobby knees, but straight, white teeth and an expression reflecting an unshaken confidence in the fairness of the universe. He was beautiful and terrible and sad. Or maybe that was just what my therapist would have called projection.

"Walter," he placed a hand on my knee. I knew what he was going to say before he said it. "Would you like me to pray for you?" He asked this in the same straightforward way one asks if you'd like a cup of water while they're up. He was on a never-ending quest to convert me, save my soul from eternal damnation. It was all right, though, because I was on a quest to convert him, too.

"Only if you kiss me, first," I raised an eyebrow suggestively.

"I'm serious," he said. "You have a hole in your life and there's only one person who can fill it."

"One person who can fill my hole? Come on, Matthew, you're making it too easy!" I laughed sucking down more wine. Matthew shook his mop of hair. He was so much younger than me he could have been my son. But he wasn't. I had no sons and neither did Matthew Zielgler. He had friends, sure, but who would carry on his legacy? Does it matter once you were gone? I started to feel even worse than before.

"Seriously, Walt, what else is bothering you? You said the funeral was only part of it, so what is it? I want to help." Matthew had stood and was tidying the stack of loose manuscript pages on my desk.

I inhaled through my nose. "The Tribune wants to run a reflection on Matthew Zeigler's life. And they asked me to write it," I breathed out.

"Oh. And you don't want to?"

"It…I don't know. What would I say? He's gone. We were in love once, or at least I was, but that was years ago. I know almost nothing about who he really was. I mean he owned a restaurant and liked overweight white guys with asthma, but that's the extent of what I know. Besides, I don't like thinking about him being dead."

"Well then don't write it. Simple," he nodded his head.

"I already said yes, that's the thing," I said, wringing my hands. "And his mother already knows about the piece and she kissed my cheek at the funeral. I still have some of the lipstick stained on there." I touched the spot gingerly, not wanting to smear it if it was still there. I groaned and sank into the deep lake of the couch. "I have to write it. I will write it. I don't want to write it. But I must."

"Okay. How much time did they give you?"

"Two days," I said. "To find out everything I need to know about Matthew Zeigler."

"I'll help," he said.

"It's a date," I said.

"Not a date," he said. "A work opportunity."

"Okay fine," I said. Matthew and I had standing appointments in our schedules set aside for writer's workshops and discussions on the one thing we saw eye to eye on: literature. Learning about a dead man is the same as learning about Chaucer, I supposed. "Have it your way. Let's get coffee tomorrow and discuss it." I finished off the wine and stalked down the hall to bed. I slipped into a troubled sleep, waking several times, seeing both Matthew's intertwined in sexual and violent embraces.

***

It was Sunday and the church rush was just kicking itself into gear. The coffee shop was a hive of conversation. I had already been there for an hour flirting with Trish, the brown haired, ponytailed barista, while Matthew was working on his relationship with God at St. Leo's down the block. I liked flirting with Trish because she knew I was gay and so we could say nasty, provocative things to each other with no repercussions or awkward tension. I had told her earlier that her ass should be the model ass for mannequins across the country. They should replace all of the asses with hers and they'd sell many more jeans.

Matthew and I always sat at a window booth. I planned it this way so I could watch the yoga class as it released next door and their tight bodies could dance across my peripheral vision. I liked to watch people who were more fit and lived better than I did. It gave me hope for the future, even if I wasn't going to be a part of it. Young people made me happy. I sat across from Matthew and he scribbled into his notebook like he was trying to start a fire from the friction.

"Are you ready for our date, dear?" I sipped my espresso.

"Listen to this, I think it's pretty good," he said setting his notebook on the table. "You said he was a chef, right?"

"Restaurateur, but close enough."

"Ok, that still works, I think." He set down his notebook and stared me right in the eyes. Opening line: Matthew Ziegler, devoted friend, packed his knives too soon." He tilted his head like a cocker spaniel, waiting for my response.

"Shit." I said.

"Really?" he said, looking at the words on the page again.

"What is that, a TV show reference? The knives bit?" I shook my head. "I don't want to talk about the article. I'm not going to write it."

"But you said you promised you would," he questioned, rolling up a sleeve. He was wearing a blue vest over his button up shirt that so many kids seemed to be doing lately.

"People break promises all the time," I said with a wave of my hand. "I just don't want to think about it. I want to think about something less depressing than dying. There's so many other things in the world."

"But Walter," he hesitated.

"But Matthew?"

"Death is just a beginning," he said finally. I raised an eyebrow. "It's not a final anything, it's a gateway into a life that is infinitely greater than this one," he was gesturing like a pastor. It was sad, really. Every Sunday he would come back from church inspired and a little depressed and would start reading the Bible out loud near me, hoping he could convert me by osmosis. It had long been my suspicion that part of him still wanted to be a priest. Wanted to save people. Unfortunately, I had to take the brunt of this mournful energy every Sunday and I received many speeches, which were objectively, often quite passionate and inspiring. I treated it like didactic beat poetry and enjoyed of it what I could. Some days, days like today, the preaching was less appreciated.

"Please, Matthew, don't preach to me today. My friend is dead and gone and someday I will be dead and gone and who will write my essay? That's what I'm thinking about." I cradled my ceramic mug in my wrinkled hands, absorbing the heat seeping through the cup. Which was magical, when I thought about it, the way heat moves through surfaces. I never thought about those types of things very much; little things that were miracles.

"I just want you to realize that you don't have to think like that, Walter. There's a better way," he said, touching the top of my hand. "You know what I'm talking about. You've heard it before, but I think today is the day we save you Walter." I stared at this new experience, this physical contact like I imagined a bird stares at a stick bug – not quite sure if it is real and so is unwilling to move in case other birds are watching and it ends up being a twig and the birds all laugh at the other bird. It was exhilarating either way.

"Enough Matthew," I said. "What is the difference between a church and a cult, anyway? Yes there is less ritualistic suicide, but you make it sound like being happy is so easy, and it's not. I know it's not because I've been alive longer than you. Trust me, being happy is not as easy as you make it seem." I finished my coffee. I caught a blue mat and perfectly formed buttocks out of the corner of my eye. It was moving slowly and so I chanced a glance: stretched lycra held it up, firm, like a sculpture of an ass. It was a man's which gave it a muscular appeal, but really it could have been either gender and it would have pleased me. It was the shapes and the tightness that drew me in. That made me want to squeeze and bite and cry and photograph them. But the buttocks passed out of my vision and I turned back to Matthew.

"Walter, I know how you feel and I don't want you to feel like I pressure you," he said, gesturing to me with his thin, clean hands. "If you would only come and confess you could see how good it feels."

"Oh? And what would I confess, preacher?" I rested my chin in my palm.

"I'm not a preacher," he said.

"Oh, trust me Matthew I am aware. I might be the only one at this table who is."

"Whatever sin you've committed, you don't have to tell me, but just getting a clean start can be so freeing. Everything will be washed away and you'll start fresh," he smiled his handsome smile.

"And what sins are those? Impure thoughts, possibly?" I winked at him. "Are you sure you are ready to hear my confession Pastor Dorman?" I ran my fingers across the table and up his wrist before he shook it away, rolling his eyes. "Oh, I'm sorry," I said retreating to my side of the table. "Did I make you uncomfortable? How un-Christian of me." He sighed into his cappuccino. He made to speak, thought better of it, then continued.

"It makes me uncomfortable that you sexualize me so often, Walter," he said staring into my chest. I was blown back in my chair. I had thought we had an understanding. He gets to preach to me, and I get to sexualize him. It was a mutually beneficial arrangement.

"It's not about your…" he paused looking to the ceiling. I crossed my arms, he was digging a grave and I was not about to reach in and haul him out. "…Lifestyle. It's just it has been happening more than usual lately and it's making me feel uncomfortable around you." He looked up at me and I stared down my nose at him. "You can't even get through a normal conversation anymore, Walter! I mean two days ago we were discussing Faulkner and all you wanted to talk about was how you thought I would make a sexy Southern dandy."

I stared at him, blown away. He would, though, I had to admit, look sexy as a Southern dandy. Yet there was no way I had been acting that out of the ordinary. He was the one who was laying on the preaching. "Trish!" In lieu of a response I called my favorite barista over as character witness.

"Another double espresso Walt?" She asked her hand on her shapely hip.

"Yes, but first, I wanted to ask you if I make you feel uncomfortable," I said, offering her to Matthew. She laughed the way waitresses and bartenders and baristas across the globe laugh when they don't know what to say.

"Lately," Matthew said patiently. She turned to him. "I expressed that Walter's particular brand of affection has made me feel uncomfortable."

Trish looked at the two of us and shrugged her shoulders apologetically. "Ah. I see. So can I get you anything Matthew?" she asked as if she'd been momentarily struck deaf and recovered just then. He declined and she walked quick back to the counter. It was like being slapped in the face. I didn't even watch her walk away. Had I really been making her feel uncomfortable? Was it the mannequin ass, thing? I felt betrayed. Matthew raised his eyebrows.

"Maybe we should get back to this article," he said, sliding the notebook back onto the table.

"And you are so much better?" I shot back, angry for being put on the spot. He was not going to come out of this unscathed and looking like John the Baptist. "This is what religion does to people. You put them in a corner and you tell them all the things they like to do are wrong and make them feel awful, then you brainwash them into thinking the way you do! Maybe you make people uncomfortable with your behavior, did you realize that? Do you even care? You don't see me staging an intervention." He ran a hand through his slicked back mop and stared out the window.

Trish came back and set my espresso lightly in front of me and backed away like she had just planted a bomb and any sound louder than a whisper would set it off. I stared into the inky darkness that could be any depth from that angle. I could fall in and disappear into it, like a wormhole and I'd be somewhere caffeinated and warm for the rest of my life. I sipped my wormhole.

"I know why you've been upset lately, Walter," Matthew said finally. He'd been checking his phone and I'd been staring out the window, waiting for more yoga students to walk by.

"Good," I said. "God call you up and chit-chat about it?"

"Your friend died, and it's awful, and now you're afraid. You're starting to think about your own mortality… which is totally natural," he assured me. "I took grief counseling at Seminary and trust me everything you're going through is part of a process. But there is a better way to deal with it."

"First of all, he wasn't my friend. He was my lover, Matthew. I'm gay, deal with that for once. Second, my friend dies and you think all I care about is myself? Is that what you think of me?" I was on the defensive but the truth was I was starting to think about death. I was going to die, someday, and I didn't know what would happen afterward. That never bothered me until Matthew Z., someone whom I had shared part of myself, had spent nights together, died from something as ordinary and unavoidable as cancer. It terrified me.

"It's all perfectly natural, everything you're feeling," he said again. "If you would just…" He bit his lip scratched his stubbly cheek.

"If I would just what? Go to church? Go to confession? Accept Jesus Christ as my Lord and Savior? That's what you were going to say, right?" I stared at him. He had sunken into his chair, defeated at last. I was still tempted. Whatever I was saying, I knew, deep down, I didn't know anything about what happens after. Neither did Matthew, I reminded myself, but I didn't, either.

"All right," I exhaled, meeting Matthew's eyes. He slid up in his seat.

"Hmmm?"

"I said all right, I'll do it, I'll go to church. What do I know? You were right, I'm scared, I drink too much and I haven't had a physical in five years. I could have cancer and I wouldn't even know." Saying it out loud made me shiver.

"Walter," he started, his eyes glistening. "I don't know what to – "

"I'll do it," I interrupted. "Only if you kiss me."

He stared at me, his face fallen blank, tears caught in their ducts.

"You heard me. You want me to go to church. I said I'll do it. If you kiss me, on the mouth, right here, in this coffee shop. In front of Trish and the rest of the world to see." I said digging my finger into the wood of the table.

"You can be a real son of a bitch, you know that?" he said through gritted teeth. "I can't believe you. Sometimes you are just too damn much, Walter."

"Can't believe what? What's my soul worth to you?" I pointed to my chest. "Don't you want me to be saved? To see you and God in heaven? Don't you want ease some of that Seminary drop-out guilt? I'm scared to die, but I shouldn't be the only one going out of their comfort zone for someone else."

"But Walter," he said, leaning over the table. His face had turned cherry red. "You know I can't do that."

"Then I guess when I die I'll be in hell with the rest of the fags and the Nazis. Should be a great fucking reunion." I slumped into the seat, turning to meet the glances of a few of the nosier customers. "Just know," I said, leaning back across the table, "that you had a chance to save someone, really save someone, and you were too afraid. It would mean nothing to you, anyway. Nothing."

"It's a sin, Walter," he was whispering now, whether out of squeamishness or privacy I hadn't a clue.

"Says who? You wouldn't enjoy it, would you? You'd be doing it to save a soul. You think God would begrudge you a peck on the lips if it meant snaring another soul for the good guys?" He blinked at me. I could see his wheels turning trying to find something to flip against it. I couldn't believe what I was concocting, myself. Saying the words had my heart pounding, my mind felt sharp as it had in years. Finally, a real conversation. Something alive. "Just admit it," I said. "You're just as scared of yourself as I am." He shrugged into his shoulder, his elbows resting on the tabletop. He stared into his coffee, probably cold by now. I clicked my tongue and leaned next to him. "I just want you to say it. Say that your squeamishness is worth the price of my soul."

He met my eyes, his pupils deep lakes reflecting a canopy of stars. The coffee grinder whirred to life somewhere beyond us. The couple at the table next to us was looking through baby pictures, oohing and ahhing. Outside it had begun to drizzle, and it pattered softly on the window. With the clouds rolling in, the coffee shop dimmed. There was nothing anymore but our two sets of eyes.

I exhaled. His head jerked forward, twisting sideways, catching me off guard. Before I could move or shift, his lips collided with mine, pressing my head back. Our teeth clanked together, a cheers with porcelain cups. I froze, not daring to move my lips, not daring to close my eyes. We stayed like that, our faces pressed together, until the beans had finished grinding and cut to silence. We separated like two cars after a high-speed collision, the bent metal of our lip fibers clinging.

He wiped his shirtsleeve across his mouth and stared at me, his jaw tensing, his breath coming in quick snorts like a rodeo bull.

I couldn't breathe. I was faintly aware that I was digging my nails into my palm.

He jerked his eyebrows up, still breathing hard through his nose. I felt a surge of fear and glanced down into my espresso, my wormhole of escape. I twirled my tiny cup, an oily whirlpool.

I finally looked up. I shook my head slowly. "Listen, Matthew, I – ," I begged with my eyes for him to understand that I couldn't do it. I didn't want him to kiss me. I realized that too late, but I didn't want him to do it, really. And I knew I'd never be accepted into a church. They'd have to bring a snack into the confessional to sit through what I had to tell. They'd burn me at the stake.

"Unfuckingbelievable," he spat, shooting out of his seat.
"Matthew," I said pathetically, trying to stand and reach him, but my knees knocked the table and my espresso flipped, the coffee splattering my lap. I went to wipe it off, and when I looked up, Matthew was a ghost and the door sighed closed.

I fell back into my seat and rested my forehead against the window, my breath fogging the glass. The yoga class filed out the door, holding their mats over their heads to stave off the rain, their perfectly shaped bodies fluttering off somewhere warm and safe. I stared at the spilled espresso that had had the audacity to stain my good chinos and tried to think of a good lie to write in Matthew Ziegler's memory.

Journey to the Sea: A Collection of Short Poems

Lorna McGinnis

<u>Ocean</u>

Rivulets like gold veins
Swim across my pied skin,

Where pockets of green and turquoise
Shiver in the crest of my breaths

And if you look down through my navy blood
You can see my cool midnight heart below.

<u>Seashell</u>
Battered and buffed
By the galloping foam,

Delicate like the turquoise
Between deep ocean and sand,

Its spiral calligraphy etched
In swooping lines,

Fresh from the sea
It sparkles like a wish.

<u>Diving Under</u>
Amber kelp tangles round my calves
As goose bumps run up my legs.

I reach down to catch the quicksilver foam
As it vanishes under the dappled water.

While the slippery sand oozes between my toes,
I watch the tumbled waves charge the shore.

Until I duck down into a cool wet world,
That begins and ends with the brine at the back of my throat.

By the Water's Edge

Water like clouded silver
Laps its way to shore
In white froths,
Smoothing the stones
To marble roundness.

A girl pauses on a wet log
Curled inwards as she stares out,
Past the place where
Sea touches sky—
With eyes like gray ocean.

Seeing a moment,
Painted into time
For the beat of a breath,
And the ripple of the wind,

Suspended in a raindrop—

Before it shatters.

Inside the Wind

I swoosh over the lake
Like the hallow breeze

That capers to the tune
Of the cawing gulls

As it whirls under my t-shirt,
Turning its sleeves to sails.

The Words in the Water

The river rustles
Like a rainmaker

Passing the lee of the hill,
With the white parsley
And the purple foxglove bells,

It winds down from its glacial home
To speak to the sea

In the prose of the currents—
Those ripples looping over its surface

Like a dead language,
Arising from the deep.

All We Know

Dawn Ellis

"Coffee's on," he says, as he sets the welcomed drink on the end table next to my side of the bed.

"Thank you. I love you," I say.

"Smell the pancakes and bacon?" he entices. "Breakfast is almost ready, Sleepyheads. That means you, too, Dog," he teases.

Dog, draped over my legs, wiggles and slaps his tail on the bed. The boy and girl are draped over my stomach, the girl rubbing my face. "You're so soft," she says. She gently tangles her fingers in my hair. The boy tickles Dog on the nose and on his neck. Dog licks him, a wet, scratchy kiss.

"Oooh, gross," the boy exclaims, delighted. "When can we go out on the beach?" he asks me, eager.

"How about after breakfast, after we clean up?" I suggest, giving us more time to be.

"Come on, Dog," the boy commands, jumping up, undeterred. "Let's get going!"

Dog, too, jumps off the bed, ready to swim for the sticks that the boy will throw, over and over.

And we ease into the day . . .

***

Look at the eagle gliding over, ducks floating on the pond near the cabin, their velvety green heads a reflection of the trees. Smell the salt water. Feel the squirt of the geoduck on our legs. Wade in

45

the water. Catch tiny crabs, and let them tickle our hands. Dig a hole; stand in it; start to sink; and jump out. Write our names in the sand with sticks. Break for lunch and dinner but feed much of our sandwiches to the seagulls and Dog.

Play until we are played out.

I pick the girl up. She is wet, sandy, tired, and I grasp the boy's hand. He lags a little behind, still bending over to turn rocks and pick up "one more shell" to add to his already-full treasure bag. Dog walks beside us . . .

***

We walk toward him.

He sits patiently, smiling, on the steps of the worn cabin deck, while the boy shows him the shells, rocks, and driftwood pieces.

The girl sits in my lap, falling in and out of sleep. We rock in the old rocker on the porch, a comfortable, threadbare quilt over her. I look at her pink baby cheeks and the boy, drifting off, leaning on his shoulder.

The full moon rises . . .

***

Full moon sliced into pieces of pie by tree branches, reminiscent of a day spent picking blackberries. I carry the bucket of berries back to the cabin and rinse away the leaf pieces and little bugs and dust. I roll out the dough and mix the berries, their heart-red juice spilling on sparkling grains of sugar. As the mixture heats, dough and berry and sugar smells fill the cabin; bubbly hot berries burst through golden brown crust.

I sit on the deck next to him, vanilla ice cream melting over the pie slices in our bowls. We blow on each spoonful, savoring the too-hot bites.

Later, we dance under the moonlight. He whisper-sings in my ear. The sand sifts through our bare toes.

Dog wades into the water's cool, wavy reflections and tries to catch the stars . . .

***

Today, I am grateful for you, Little Dipper and Big Dipper, and other constellations that light our way. Let them guide us when we are lost. I am grateful for you, Dog, the pie, the shells, the rocks, driftwood pieces, the sand. Thank you for the children, oh, the children, and him. Let this summer night's breeze gently whisper away hurts, and let us always feel the cool touch of hope.

Thank you for the trials that have led us to a confluence of love and a wearing down, the calm, quiet wisdom that comes only from heartbreak, loneliness, and lost dreams. Now, we move away from worry and toward the phosphorescence of the shells at the water's edge at eventide, and the heron squawking its prehistoric cry of all that has come before.

Today, I am grateful, especially for knowing that everything comes out in the end . . .

***

Everything. I pull the girl child in, tucking the quilt tighter around her, protective of her smallness. He holds the sleeping boy child.

I look at him. Our eyes meet and speak of all we know . . .

Ostrich

Dan Rahe

In 1990, my father bought four ostriches -- two breeding pairs. We lived on an old dairy farm, and dad and I had retrofitted the barns and pastures, which were perfectly adequate for habitation by placid bovines, to make them suitable for giant, speedy African avians. Ostrich farming was something of a fad in the late 1980's and early 1990's, and many enterprising farmers had made a small fortune from hide and meat sales. My dad, being the kind of person who suspects the path to success is cleverly hidden, studied ostrich husbandry with zeal, and eventually arranged to have some delivered to our Minnesota farmstead.

The four ostriches who lived within view of my second story bedroom window represented a welcome maturation of Dad's financial risk-taking. His previous "investment" misadventure had been as a Greeting Cards Entrepreneur, and boxes of them still occupied a large portion of our homeschool learning space. In theory, my father was supposed to work out deals with gas stations, truck stops, and gift stores for the display and sales of these off-brand greetings, but they never sold very well, because they were fucking awful. These cards were printed on high-gloss stock, and were written with all the humor and sensitivity of an excessively sober art school dropout who might list Jim Belushi as a muse. Every color was too vivid, and every hackneyed sentiment was expressed without a shred of subtlety.

The cards embarrassed me. But worse still, since we possessed literally THOUSANDS of them, on special occasions, we never went to the Hallmark store or the main street druggist to purchase, you know, normal people cards. So, on my friends' birthdays, I'd have to thumb through all these wretched, ham-fisted, sickly gleaming wastes of my college fund to find the least humiliating drivel to send them. Sometimes I intentionally moved the boxes of cards right up against the baseboard heaters, hoping maybe they'd catch fire and be disposed of. "That's awful, Dad," I imagined myself saying, as if there were ever enough idiots in the entire county to comprise a legitimate market for that tripe.

Yes, the ostriches were better than the greeting cards. Even so, I knew somewhere in the back of my mind that this was another purchase my father had made by flailing in the dark, fueled by a misguided hope of financial bliss. Maybe he wanted his six older brothers to make the drive up from their successful dairy collectives in Iowa, just to see how well-off their kid brother had gotten by chasing his dreams. Maybe that was it. I was only eleven years old, but I knew things probably weren't going to turn out the way Dad hoped. He worked so hard though, and worked me so hard, I couldn't help but question my pragmatic doubts. Every fencepost hole I dug and every pound of bird shit I wheeled out of the barn was an investment in my dad and his dreams. The birds -- the giant damn birds -- meant nothing to me. It was not an adventure, and they were not my pets.

Try as you might, there is no way to establish a connection or rapport with an ostrich. They are very tall -- nearly 8 feet -- which makes it difficult for them to maintain meaningful eye contact with you. Also, they are quite gawky, and never seem to reconcile with their own bodies, awkwardly heaving the massive bulk of their torso about on spindly, haphazard legs, with their clueless heads bobbing around like an afterthought on their dirty-gym-sock necks. They carry themselves as if continually astounded by their surroundings, and their wide, long-lashed eyes highlight that impression. For an ostrich, life is a very confusing thing, and they don't seem to be able to make space for relational bonds in their quest to simply survive each hour.

No, an ostrich is not majestic or exotic in the least, not after a week or so of daily interaction anyway. They carry a distinct odor of heavy dander due to the flaky quarter-inch-thick quills of their feathers and their dry skin. They defecate with alarming frequency, and it is as jarring as a sudden accidental birth every time: a half-gallon spew of milky white urine splashes to the ground, followed by dense plum-sized turds. In the winter, the ostriches were often frightened by the steam rising from their own fresh mess, and would flee from it in a state of panic, stupid heads drawn back like some kind of voodoo Muppet, crashing into anything and everything in their inscrutable path.

In such a condition of unbridled fear, the ostrich is a dangerous creature, if not for their 300-pounds, then even more for the claw extending from the larger of their two toes like a sharpened hoof. For this reason, once the birds reached sexual maturity, we kept very respectful distances from them. A being equipped with inadequate intellect, lethal weapons, and frustrated sexuality is a thing to be avoided.

To survive in the African desert, ostriches are well-equipped for environmental extremes, but the desert is a far cry from the bone-chilling cold of Minnesota winters. It can be quite comical to watch the birds frolic in knee-deep snow, with icicles hanging from their eyelashes. To keep them from freezing, each sunset, I would carefully herd them into the barn, pull the twelve-foot high doors shut, and light two propane-fueled patio heaters. The ostriches would settle on the floor, which was covered with eight inches of sand, and watch me turn out the lights with uncomprehending interest.

By the time I was 15, our flock of ostriches had swelled to over 60, with chicks, juveniles, and adult birds scattered about the ten acres of our quaint Victorian-era outpost. Once a year, Dad would rent a horse trailer, and we'd haul a few unsuspecting yearlings off to be slaughtered for their feathers, meat, and hide. Corralling ostriches is a difficult task. They can run forty miles an hour, and are prone to panic. The only way to calm them is to cover their eyes, because ostriches subscribe to the belief that what they can't see isn't happening. This is accomplished usually by cornering the bird and covering its head with a snug sack -- a technique we called "socking."

I like to think that I was a talented ostrich farmer. I knew each one on the farm by its markings or habits, and was eventually able to run the entire enterprise with little help from Dad. But one day in January, I noticed a younger male, who was nearly fully grown but without the black feathers of maturity, who did not join the others at the feeding trough. He lurked in the back of the barn and watched the others in their morning feeding frenzy: their beaks scooping mouthfuls from the trough, then jerking their heads backwards like a person swallowing a pill. You could watch the fist-sized wads of food sliding down inside their necks. Six hours later, when it came time for the evening feeding, the lone male still showed no interest in food.

The next day, he did not eat. He didn't seem sluggish, or visibly ill. He ran in the deep snow with the same stupid gusto he always had. But I was concerned, and separated him from the rest of the flock, in case he had a communicable disease.

I told Dad about the young male and his loss of appetite. Dad, in turn, called one of his ostrich farming mentors for advice. He told me that if the bird didn't eat, we would have to force feed him. I had force-fed many sickly ostrich chicks before but never a nearly-adult, otherwise healthy bird, and I was not eager to. It was the kind of endeavor that could end in severe injury to farmer, livestock, or both.

After four days without food, the young ostrich began to take more frequent rests and did not venture as often out of the barn. He even spurned water. Dad decided the time had come to attempt an intervention. It happened to be the coldest day of the year, -30 F, and the wind was blowing hard. Dad and I drove to Waconia for supplies. At Hank's Hardware, we bought eight feet of clear plastic tubing, one inch diameter, and a pipe fastener; at Mackenthun's grocery, a funnel, six cans of vanilla Ensure Adult Nutrition Beverage, and six quarts of Lemon-Lime Gatorade. Then, we got back in our 1985 F-150, which we left running in the parking lot with the heat on maximum blast, and drove back home.

I brought the Ensure Adult Nutrition Beverage and Lemon-Lime Gatorade to the kitchen, and followed Dad's recipe: Two cans of Ensure, and one-and-a-half bottles of Gatorade, mixed in a sealable gallon container. At his workbench in the barn, Dad affixed the funnel to the tubing. I carried the liquid mix out to the barn at a full run. We needed to act quickly, before the life-saving nutrient beverage froze. The ailing ostrich lay in the corner of his solitary corral, and watched us enter without rising. Dad reached out to hand me the jug of Gator-sure, and proposed a plan:

"Alright. Let's hope he stays down. You get on top of him - straddle him. I'll force his beak open and shove about 36 inches of this tube down his throat. I'll do my best to hold his head still. Then, you grab the funnel and start pouring the mix down, ok? It'll be all I can do to keep his head steady."

I adjusted the scarf around my face, because the condensation from my breath had frozen solid in the wool. "Ok," I said. "Let's get it over with."

The ostrich was too weary to move, and did not seem terribly perturbed when I put the weight of my body on him. I put my hands around his neck. But when Dad began to pry at his beak, the poor creature suddenly came to life. He tried to stand, and I leaned forward, jamming my elbows down hard against his rib cage, a motion which required me to let go of his neck. "Keep him down!" Dad shouted. His scarf had come loose, exposing his face to the cold. His grip on the bird's head was vice-like, and his jaw set with desperate determination. Unfortunately for both of us, my 140 pound frame was not sufficient to keep an angry ostrich down. I jumped to one side, and tackled him, throwing my arms around his long neck. He lurched violently against the sheet metal of the barn wall. Again, Dad tried and failed to insert the tube. The nutrient mix was already beginning to freeze. We gave up.

My heart was pumping behind my eardrums, and my face was braced against the subzero temperature in a squinting grimace. I couldn't feel my hands, and there was saliva frozen to my chin. Dad turned away from me without speaking. He began devising a new plan.

He sent me up to the house to fetch a space heater to keep the Gatorade mixture warm. When

I returned, he was standing on a step-ladder in the corral. "We're not gonna try to keep him down anymore," he explained. "We're just gonna get him in a corner, then I'll climb up here to tube him."

This new plan was employed with success, but it was still a pretty dicey situation resembling a weird rodeo act. From his perch on the rickety old ladder, my father tried to keep the bird's head still while I pressed from behind to keep him in the corner. The mix sloshed in the jug as I clung to it, and I could hear ice crystals brushing its plastic sides. Dad grunted, "Got it!" and signaled for me to pass him the jug. It was a tricky hand-off, and I took a blow from the ostrich's knee but held my ground, digging my cheap Sorrell knock-off boots into the sand for footing. With remarkable balance and focus, Dad poured the gallon into the funnel. The bird made a sick gurgling sound and continued his flailing resistance, but we were relentless. Dad threw the empty jug to the ground in triumph.

"We've saved a life," I thought. I wanted to get out of the cold. It was miserable, and the stinging in my toes had become unbearable.

Dad began to pull the tubing out, slowly. Half of the length came out, and the bird was still greatly agitated. Another six inches... and then, blooshhhh -- the ostrich tilted his head back and vomited forcefully straight upward. Ensure and Gatorade rained down on us from above as he twirled away and wagged his head side to side in panic. The force-feeding tube sailed across the barn and Dad nearly fell backward off the ladder. I ran, with slimy lemon-scented vomitus dripping from my gloved hands. The ostrich continued spewing the entire gallon of liquid, and it splashed down the barn walls and froze in strange patterns resembling breaking waves.

I climbed over the gate and stood outside the corral with Dad. He stared forward unblinking, seething. "Dammit," he said, through his teeth. There was ice on his mustache. "God dammit, we have to try again." So, we repeated the force-feeding procedure, this time leaving the tube in for a bit longer. Our efforts were met with another drenching and demoralizing puke incident. We abandoned our efforts to save the ostrich, and staggered to the warmth of the house.

Only a few hours later, the ostrich was dead of starvation and exhaustion.

A great beast that only hours before had been capable of killing me was now laid low on the sand, neck stretched flat out before his sadly shrugged wings, head lolled to the side. Warm Gatorade bubbled out of his beak in his final breath and left a small iced-over puddle in the sand.

Death was not a new thing to me, because it is a daily part of farm life. I knew decay and it's all-shrouding odor. Because the eggs of an ostrich are a curiosity coveted by crafting enthusiasts (hot-glue-gun slingers, silk floristry mongers, bric-a-brac fiends), my parents often ordered me to empty the contents of failed ostrich pregnancies. In practice, this meant that I would take an egg that had been lovingly warmed and rotated in a robotic incubator for weeks, with a viable embryo inside, and drill a hole in its shell with an electric Black & Decker. When the internal membrane was punctured, sulfur and methane rushed to my nose -- the smell of a dead chick, entombed in the nutrients nature had provided for its nourishment. With vigorous, careful rhythm, I'd shake the fluid out of the egg through the small hole I had just drilled, hearing the corpse of the chick thud and tumble softly inside. Gossamer bones. Then, I'd slip the end of needle-nosed pliers inside the egg, and, bit by bit, pull the sad dead baby ostrich out through the tiny hole. Sulfur, methane, ammonia. Weird blood. Wet feather down.

But this great big animal dead on the sand in my barn was something different, something I had never encountered before. As I learned in the five hours that followed, it was also something my father had never encountered.

By then, the sun had set. Somehow it became even colder. If you have experienced air colder than -30 Fahrenheit, you know that it is a physical thing -- you become conscious of every organ in your body (the material sense of them, that they are something like skin inside you, that they are woefully vulnerable) and the air feels real in a concrete and unforgiving way. It is your enemy.

Dad knelt beside the dead ostrich and shoved it with his elbow.

"He's going to freeze solid. We need to get the hide off of him before that happens," he said, without looking at me. He was quiet, his jaw twitching and the veins at his temples throbbing red. I didn't know what to do. I pulled at my stupid red stocking cap, the one I'd worn since I was 12. I was suddenly a little afraid. The red stocking cap was stitched with blue snowflakes.

With the angry tantrum-like resignation peculiar to fathers, Dad grabbed a fistful of feathers near the bird's spine, and pulled them out. "Get a bag, dammit. Get a big garbage bag. We need to get these feathers out while his body is still warm! Hurry!"

Dad still wouldn't look at me. I ran to the workbench and brought the box of black plastic bags to his side. I opened one with a grand unfurling motion. Dad took it from me roughly, still without looking at me.

"Aren't you going to help me? Goddammit, if we don't get these feathers out while the body's warm, the hide is ruined. We have to fucking hurry," he said. I'd never seen him spit so much while talking, and I'd only heard him say the "f" word once before. I recoiled like a child, even though I was 15, even though I'd just tackled a fucking ostrich a few hours earlier.

Now, I have a son of my own and he is 13 years old. When he assists me with household chores, he hangs back and never commits to the task -- not out of laziness, but out of fright. I can tell he fears that these seemingly simple routines -- mowing the lawn, pulling weeds, using an oven -- may have an impossible element that can only be dealt with by someone with uncommon skill. Everything about self-sufficiency is complex and mysterious to him. I know this because the same halting reach of the arms, and the same gape-mouthed subservient expression, and the same sleepwalking slowness came from me, in that moment, with my father in the barn.

He looked at me, finally, and his eyes were cold and blank. I wasn't his son anymore. We were two nearly hypothermic men shivering in a barn with an ostrich corpse, and that was all.

We pulled feathers with mad haste. Every last feather came out of that damn bird's hide while he was still warm. And my god, I never said a word. I was scared shitless, because my father was scared. Any harm that could befall me in that barn that night, I knew, would be collateral damage in a fearful and uncertain hurricane swirling inside him. We were on our own, separate but together in the dark solid cold with a dead African bird.

The matter of removing the hide from the corpse was decidedly more complex than de-feathering it. The only knives we had were kitchen knives or box-cutters, and we had no rack from which to suspend the carcass for proper dressing. We improvised, and the scant, quavering orange lights in the barn cast shadows that made all the madcap insufficiencies seem macabre.

We tied ropes to the ostrich's ankles, and hoisted it from the rafters until his beak scraped the floor in pendulous arcs. More Gatorade and Ensure seeped from his mouth. I don't remember his eyes. We took turns then: One of us would cut at the hide and peel it from the carcass while the other warmed his hands by the space heater -- because it is a bad thing to be handling a knife near an expensive hide when one has lost all sensation in his fingers. It was laborious to scrape so carefully with the cursed little box cutter blades at such a surprisingly thick skin, feeling the corpse becoming progressively less warm with every minute. If the flesh froze, the hide would be ruined.

We peeled back the skin from the ostrich's torso quickly, if not skillfully, and I hope to never do such a thing again. But to remove the hide in one singular, market-ready piece, we needed to get to the smooth flesh of the bird's thigh. With his head on the ground, followed by nearly four feet of neck and three feet of torso, the thighs and knees were suspended well above our heads. So, to remove the entire hide, we would need to lower the bird from its hoisted position by a foot or two.

We untied the anchoring knots and tried to lower the ostrich a bit, but his neck was frozen stiff. His half-flayed corpse pivoted clumsily on his head, four feet of neckmeat refusing to yield.

I think Dad must have known, then, what we would have to do next, but wasn't willing to articulate it. Or perhaps he didn't know. Perhaps this setback was insurmountable in his mind, for a minute. I couldn't tell. I fucking stayed silent while he Full-on Lost His Shit. He stabbed the bird's carcass with the box-cutter knife with one raging blow and sent it swinging. He kicked the space heater, punted it across the barn. I tied off my anchor line and ran to the retrieve the space heater, because I needed it. My hands were dead. I needed it.

When your hands come back to life after they are dead, the sting is pretty tremendous. I slapped my thighs to hurry the return of blood to my fingers. God dammit god dammit goddammit it was cold.

There was still time to remove the hide, still time to make this bird worth the money we had invested in his existence. But there was only one thing to do, and it was, by far, the least pleasant thing I have ever been asked to do.

We needed to behead the ostrich.

I retrieved a circular saw from Dad's workbench, because he didn't own a chainsaw and because a handsaw would have been too slow. Dad held the massive bird steady while I cut, first through tiny gray ethereal neck feathers, then through the respiratory, circulatory, and digestive vessels. Frozen blood and coagulated tissue spat from the sides of the cruel saw, and I wanted to stop because it seemed so disgusting and senseless. Why did I need to do this?

That thought came and went like the last ebb of a low tide. My moral dilemma was only seconds long, because I was in pain from the cold and because I loved my Dad and because I was horribly afraid of my Dad. When the blade sliced clean through, at last, the ostrich's neck tipped and fell aside, with an audible "plunk" on the floor like a loosened table leg.

It was 5 o'clock in the morning of the next day before Dad and I were done dressing that bird and cleaning up.

University of Minnesota veterinary students drove to our farm a few hours later to take the carcass in for study. They determined that the bird had died because its intestines were twisted. Nothing could get through the digestive tract, like a kinked garden hose.

We never talked about that ordeal after it happened. Now, my father only faintly recalls that such a thing occurred. But for the love of bleeding Jesus, I will never forget the day I cut an ostrich's head off with a goddamn circular saw.

The Observable Universe

Jonny Eberle

The young man buys a ticket and wanders around the exhibit on the history of the spacesuit before disappearing. It takes more than forty minutes before the observatory volunteers find him locked in the Clark Telescope Dome. He refuses to come out.

The man demands to know why he can't see Saturn through the telescope's eyepiece. He doesn't believe them when they explain through the closed door that the rotation of the Earth has shifted the planet out of the telescope's field of view. They offer to come inside and reposition the telescope for him. He tells them that he is not a fool. That he will wait.

"I want to see her fly through Saturn's rings on her way out." He says this three times in quick succession. They assure him that they understand, but exchange worried glances.

The volunteers fetch the astronomer who is about to leave for Happy Jack to watch an alien world transit in front of its star five hundred light years away.

"This planet is in a highly elliptical orbit," he tells them, dropping a bottle of bourbon into the passenger seat of his hatchback. "It may not cross the plane of the star again in my lifetime."

But they explain that the telescope is historic and they fear the man might try to hurt it in some way. The astronomer caves, grabs his bottle and agrees to talk to the intruder.

"Really, this one isn't all that interesting," the astronomer says through the locked door. He shivers under the whispering pine trees. "The one you really want to see is the one behind the rotunda. That's the one that discovered Pluto.

"I have no interest in dwarf planets," the man says calmly. "I want to swim in the canals on Mars."

"There are no canals on Mars," the astronomer sighs, shaking his head.

"Lowell sat right where I'm sitting now and he saw them."

The astronomer goes on to explain that the canals were an illusion; liquid water has long since frozen under the surface and the planet is currently lifeless.

"Like this one," the man murmurs.

The astronomer instructs the volunteers, a retired middle school biology teacher and a painfully awkward college freshman girl who reads manga on her breaks, to go back to the visitor center and call the police.

"It's just you and me now," the astronomer says, leaning into the door. "No one's going to hurt you."

"How long does it take for a human body to break down into its constituent atoms?"

"Hell if I know," the astronomer says. "A long time."

"And then, those atoms could recombine in the heart of a star, could become alive again on a distant world?"

"Yeah, I guess that could happen. It's a big universe."

"I want to press myself through the lens," the man whispers. His voice echoes through the cavernous interior of the white dome. "I want to fire myself out of this telescope like it were a cannon."

"Where would you go?" the astronomer asks. He slides down the wall to sit on the sidewalk.

"All the places I used to go before," the man says, as if this were obvious. The astronomer can tell from the hushed tone of the man's voice that he is looking out of the slit in the roof, at the stars that burn in the moonless night. It makes everyone speak more softly. Somewhere in the firmament of stars, a distant sun is rising over a distant planet and the astronomer will not be there to see it. He decides to drink the whole bottle of bourbon tonight.

They sit in silence, watching the galaxy turn, for another ten minutes before the police officers come up the path with the volunteers. The five of them huddle out of earshot of the man, beside the mausoleum where the observatory's founder is buried.

The man's car is in the parking lot. Its plates match those of a vehicle involved in a hit and run accident on Route 66 a couple of hours ago. A teenage girl is dead. The officers saw blood on the front bumper.

"He's having a mental breakdown in there," the college student says.

"I think he's high on bath salts," the teacher chimes in.

The two officers approach the dome. They have their guns drawn. One of them is shaking, either from the cold or fear of what kind of man waits in the dark for them.

"Police! Open up," the shaky one demands.

"Life on Earth only exists for a fraction of a second of cosmic time, you know," the man replies. "So small. So fragile."

The officers whisper to each other. They're going to break down the door. There is an outburst from the volunteers. The door is part of the original structure, built in 1896. The astronomer tells them to go ahead and break it down, but not to shoot the telescope.

The door is sturdier than anyone expects. It takes three tries for them to crack the frame around the deadbolt. All the while, the man inside is silent. The officers enter the dome, shouting for the man to put his hands on his head and come out where they can see him. The astronomer peeks his head inside — the man is not there. The officers are circling around the small dome, searching high and low.

"Is there another way out?" the shaking one asks the volunteers. There isn't. The second officer radios that the man has somehow escaped. They don't report that he vanished into the thin night air.

The astronomer follows the telescope's sleek silver body with his eyes and thinks how much it does look like a cannon. He wonders if the man will go swim in the canals of Mars or if he will first watch the girl fly from the bumper of his car up through the rings of Saturn.

Ride Along

Jack Cameron

The shotgun blast was so loud that it took me a moment to even understand what I'd just done. I can't say for sure what I was feeling. There was anger. There was fear. But most of all, there was a strange giddiness. If it hadn't been my first time firing a shotgun, maybe it would have felt differently. The two men in front of me looked at me in disbelief. One of them had just the hint of a grin when the other one fell. And though I knew I was done, I was ready to fire again.

The previous night, there was no shotgun. My only weapon was a heavily used blue nylon jacket with the word 'Security' embroidered on the upper left hand side, like a nametag. My job was simple: stand outside the Food Mart from 6pm to midnight. That was it. If the place got robbed, I was supposed to call 911, like any customer would do. If someone stole something, I was to tell Todd, the night manager. I was a grocery store scarecrow. My training consisted of being told where to punch my time card and where to hang up the jacket that had been worn by countless security guys before me. Twice a night (at 9pm and at 11pm), an armed rent a cop would drop by while Todd did a safe drop. My first night on shift, the rent a cop said to me, "You're just a deterrent. I'm the stopper." He patted his holstered pistol for effect.

The job was Lisa's idea. Lisa was the sort of girlfriend who looked at boyfriends like projects. She knew that I wanted to be a cop. At 19, I was still two years away from being eligible for the Washington State Academy. I'd taken a criminology course at Tacoma Community College, but now was summer. Sure it was boring, but it was a job. And as Lisa often reminded me, " Nick…a lot of being a cop is standing around doing nothing." And money was money. Even if it wasn't much.

Most nights, I didn't mind the monotony. I'd joke around with the cashiers and help them take down the outdoor fruit displays at closing time. But that night, I didn't want to be there. Lisa was at a party and even though it was with her lesbian friend, Rose and that whole crowd, I'd rather have been there. Lisa thought she was being the good girlfriend by sending me texts on my cell telling me how much she missed me, but really all it did was make me want to walk off the job.

By the time midnight came around, I was more than ready to leave. It'd been another uneventful night. The most exciting thing that happened that night was Todd throwing out a drunk who'd managed to throw up in the vegetable aisle.

I exchanged texts with Lisa, while I walked the mile back to our basement apartment.

Me: I M OFF U STILL @ R's?

Lisa: No. I'm home now. Stop using text speak.

Me: BUT WE R TXTING

Lisa: And you're still literate. Type like a human.

Me: Okay. You win.

Lisa: I always do.

Me: LUV U

Lisa: Come home so I can beat you properly.

I was home before one, but Lisa was sleeping. My least favorite aspect of my job wasn't the hours. It was that I seemed to miss everything. Nine times out of ten after work sex wasn't an option because Lisa was already asleep. I went into the bedroom, got undressed listening to her quiet snoring, and went to bed.

***

The knock on the door woke us both up. There were three quick hard knocks. Basement apartments tend to have this thing where every sound in the place echoes. I grabbed some dirty clothes off the floor. I caught a quick glimpse of Lisa's breasts as she got up and went down the hall to the bathroom. I saw her naked every day, but I loved those brief accidental peaks. I opened the front door and was not ready for what was on the other side.

At first I thought he was a stripper, but the uniform and gun were too real. Still, the Elvis Presley shades and the slicked back black hair almost defused any authority the guy might have. He chewed gum like it was tobacco. He looked me up and down and said, "You gotta be Nick. I'm Dean."

Maybe it was too early. Or maybe I wouldn't have known what to say regardless of what time it was. I got out an, "Um…"

"This is 2010 Proctor. Apartment 1. Right?"

"Yeah." The cop stood there for a moment with a look that said, 'Is this the right place?'

"Oh shit. She didn't tell you." The cop said.

"Tell me what?"

"Lisa. That's your girlfriend, right? She set you up for a ride along. Get dressed man."

What. The. Fuck. "I'll be right back." I shut the door.

Lisa walked into the living room wearing a bathrobe. "Lisa, there's a cop here. He says you signed me up for a ride along. Says his name's Dean. You know anything about this?"

"Crap!" Lisa said, "I totally spaced it. Sorry. Where is he?"

"He's at the door."

"You didn't invite him in?"

"No, I don't know him and he looked kinda sketchy even with the cop uniform. "

"Dean's fine. I met him and his wife at Rose's party last night."

I opened the door and let Dean in while I got ready. Twenty minutes and a quick kiss from Lisa later, I was walking out to Dean's patrol car. I got into the passenger seat and noticed the mounted laptop facing the driver's side separating the two sides of the car. Dean got in and pointed at a switch between us near the dash.

"You see this switch? This unlocks the shotgun." He pointed to the rack directly behind our heads. "You see me get into trouble, don't try to work the radio or anything. Just flip that switch, take the shotgun, and shoot the fucker."

He shifted the car into gear while I thought about whether or not 'He told me to shoot the fucker' would be a viable defense in court. We got to a stop light. Next to us I heard the familiar summer sound of some moron's bass speakers. Generally it was something I tuned out, hearing it a hundred times a night at work. But it wasn't even seven in the morning and they were blasting their radio like they were at a club. I looked over at the driver who couldn't have been older than I was. His eyes got wide and he turned it down. It took a moment for me to figure it out and when I did, I thought, 'Hey, being in a cop car has its advantages.'

We drove without saying anything. He sent a few texts with his cell and called someone at the station to tell them he had a ride along today. When he was done he said, "It's a weekday so it'll probably be boring as shit, but I'll arrest somebody. Try to make it interesting for you."

Jesus. Right now there was someone who was walking around not knowing that by the end of the day they'd be arrested for my own amusement. I thought cops arrested people because they were criminals. I kept these thoughts to myself. No reason to get on his bad side. Dean smiled at me and rounded a corner. Tires squealing.

We went down 30th Street Hill, which took us through Old Town, then hit the freeway, eventually getting off on the Tacoma Mall exit. Until a few years ago, the main police station was part of the County City Building in downtown Tacoma. Then one of those warehouse grocery stores decided to move and expand and in exchange for the permits, they sold their old place to the city of Tacoma for cheap.

As soon as we pulled into the parking lot of the station, Dean lost his sunglasses and gum. I walked into the squad room with him and no one gave me a second look. Dean disappeared and came back a few moments later with some paperwork.

"On the part that says, why you're here, just say you're interested in law enforcement. Make sure you sign everywhere you need to."

While I filled out the paperwork, I heard the sergeant, a bald, older black man, tell us about a shooting that happened last night only a couple miles from the Food Way. I wondered if I heard the shots. If I did, I hadn't noticed. The guy who got shot survived and the shooter was still out there. The suspect's description was a white guy in his twenties with a Mohawk and a neck tattoo. Obviously not a criminal mastermind. I signed the last page and handed it to Dean. "Great." He said. "Let's get out of here."

Dean offered me a stick of gum as he got back in the car. I didn't take it. He tossed a couple of pieces in his mouth and put his sunglasses back on.

"So, Nick. Why you wanna be a cop?"

"I like the idea of helping people."

Dean pulled into traffic, heading into downtown.

"Bullshit."

"What?"

"You may want to help people. That's fine. But there's only two reasons to be a cop: Either you've never had authority and you want some or you've been a bully all your life and you want to keep being a bully. Me? I won't lie. I'm the bully. What about you, Nick?"

"Like I said. I just want to help people."

"Then you should be a doctor or something, dude because I'll tell you this one for free: Cops don't help people. Most of the time, all we're doing is dealing with people no one else wants to deal with. We're garbage men."

"So if that's what it's about, what's the appeal?"

"Two things, man: One, I got the power. People talk a good game, but nobody fucks with cops. And the guys that do, we take- Whoa. Did you see that shit?"

I did. The Mazda in front of us had gone right through a red light. There was no traffic going across so we followed him through the light as Dean flipped on his lights and sirens. The car pulled over after a half block or so. Dean typed a few things into the laptop.

"The car's clean. This probably isn't anything but a dumbass. Still, stay in the car." I watched him step out and thought of all the highway patrol reality shows I'd seen where things started out just like this and then went terribly wrong. Nothing like that happened. Five minutes later, Dean walked back with a smile on his face.

"You didn't give him at a ticket?" Dean got back in the car. The Mazda drove off and a small hand waved out the driver's side.

"Her. I didn't give *her* a ticket. And if you'd have seen her, you'd understand why."

"So some girl runs a light and she gets a pass because she's hot. What if a guy like me runs the light?"

"You'd be a hundred nine-teen dollars poorer."

"That's not cool, man."

"Sure it is. Like I said, two things. The first one is power. The second one is pussy. Now don't look at me like that. I ain't one of those creeps who lets girls off for sleeping with him. That ain't right. I just give'em my number." I was sure that Lisa had mentioned something about Dean having a wife, but this didn't seem to be the best time to bring that up.

The police scanner chirped. Dean picked up the call and ten minutes later we were at an apartment building near the city dump. There was already another police car there. The building was a single level nine unit structure that looked like it might once have been a bad motel. There were broken windows and half the doors were open or missing. It looked as if it were waiting to be demolished. As we pulled up, a uniformed cop got out of his car.

Dean and I got out into the summer heat. No wonder the cop had stayed in his air-conditioned car until we arrived. Dean introduced me to the other cop. His name was Dan Salvatore. He was in his mid-30s, balding, and had more of a belly on him than I'd expect a good cop to have. His face was soft and round. He looked more like a pastor than a cop.

"What are we doing here?"

"Nick, this is a place where bad things happen." Dan said.

"Sometimes we find stolen cars here. Maybe some junkies shooting up. You never know. I've been on the force three years and Dan here shows me one of these places about once a week. These are places you've probably driven by a hundred times without really noticing. Dan here notices everything."

We walked through an open door. The door had a '5' on it. The unit was about twelve feet by ten feet. In one corner there was a bathroom that had a sink and toilet. There were empty 40 oz. bottles and cigarette butts on the ground. In the middle of the room there was a mattress that was so torn up, it was barely recognizable.

"We ever get any rape calls here?" Dean asked. Dan shook his head.

"Great place for one though. Probably only a matter of time." I would have said something, but nothing in my experience had a response for 'great place for a rape'. We heard something outside and walked back out.

The little girl couldn't have been more than two. A diaper with at least one load of crap was the only thing the kid had on. She had a red popsicle in her hand. And she was walking out of one of the open doors of what I thought was an abandoned building. I took a step towards her, but Dan held me back.

"Amber!" Dan said. "It's Officer Dan." At first I thought he was talking to the girl, but a moment later there was some commotion inside one of the units. A stringy haired blonde in a dirty tank top walked out and sneered at us.

"What you want, 'Officer Dan'?"

"You living here now, Amber?" Amber reached in her pocket, pulled out a smoke, and lit it.

"Well, y'know." She said. "The rent's cheap." She smiled a smile that was missing a few teeth.

"It looks like little Ashley needs a change. You got any diapers here?"

She glared. "Don't you worry about Ashley. I take care of my kid. Now fuck off. All a' you!"

Dan gave a nod to Dean. Dean walked past Dan and me and right up to Amber.

"Remember me, Amber?"

"Yeah, I remember you." She blew some smoke at him.

"You may have Dan there wrapped around your little skeletal finger, but I know you got a warrant out for solicitation and I think little Ashley would be better off in foster care than with your junkie ass." Dean snatched the cigarette out of her hand and let it drop to the ground.

Amber's attitude disappeared. She walked away from Dean and picked up Ashley, who smiled at her. She walked back over by Dean.

"What- what do you want?"

"We're cops, Amber. All we want to do is take down bad guys. You point us towards something worse than your warrant. We'll leave you and little Ashley alone for now."

Amber looked at Dan. He gave her nothing but a stare.

"Check number eight or nine."

"What's over there?" Dan said.

"I don't know. I stay away from it. Some Mexicans stay there sometimes."

Dean started walking towards the other units. I followed him. Dan stayed with Amber. I heard Dan say, "You gotta get a new diaper on Ashley."

Once we were out of earshot, Dean said, "That's Dan's biggest problem. He spent five years as a social worker before joining the TPD. He doesn't just want to police. He wants to solve everyone's problems. I was once at a domestic with him where, I shit you not, he helped them figure out their finances. We were there for three hours."

We walked past number six and seven and into number eight. It looked just like the one we had been in before with the exception that the right wall was destroyed leading into nine. There were a couple of chairs, a bunch of jars of something, a few rolls of tin foil, and a small fan near the window. It was about twenty degrees hotter inside than it was outside. Dean and I were already pouring sweat. As we walked into number nine through the wall, I noticed broken batteries and a camp stove. It smelled like the place had been flooded with cat piss.

Dean grabbed my arm. "We gotta get out of here."

We went to the door, but it was closed and wouldn't budge. We walked back through the wall and out the door of number eight. I felt light headed.

"What was that?"

"That was a meth lab. We gotta call the Hazmat Team." For some reason, though I'd seen junkies before, the word 'lab' always made me think that meth labs were clean or at least organized places. Having just walked through one, I realized how silly that was.

Dean and I walked over to Dan. Amber was in the back of his car with Ashley.

"You arresting her?" Dean said.

"No. I'm taking her to the grocery store. Find anything?"

"Yeah. There's a meth lab back there. I'll stick around and wait for Hazmat. You go do your good deed for the day."

Dan grinned. "Thanks Dean. She just needs a little help." Dan got in his car and drove away.

Dean and I got back to the car and he called in the meth lab.

"Hazmat teams have it made, man." Dean said.

"Why?"

"They get a call, they get three hours double overtime even if it's a false alarm."

"Not bad."

"The team won't be here for a while. Let's find a spot in the shade." Dean shifted the car into gear, but we went backwards and hit something. We looked back and saw a telephone pole. He pulled forward. We got out to inspect the damage and my head spun. There was a small mark on the bumper.

"Dude," Dean said, "I am fucked up on those fumes. How about you?"

I nodded. We got back in the car, turned on the air conditioner, and waited. Sitting with a contact high with a cop was a surreal experience. A half hour later, two vans showed up. Dean got out and talked to them for a few minutes. By then I felt a good deal better. He got back in the car and I saw the Hazmat guys getting into their moon suits.

"Dean, we were just walking through there with nothing!"

"That's why we have you sign those release forms. You could get brain damage, but you can't sue us." Dean laughed. "Let's go."

The next call we took was a burglar alarm. "Let me guess," I said, "Nine times out of ten, it's a false alarm."

"More like 9,999 out of 10,000. I've never answered a real burglar alarm and I don't know any cops who have." We got to the house and looked around. Nothing seemed out of place. He called into the alarm company and we left.

A little later there was word of a high speed chase on the radio, but by the time we got there, the show was over. The car was pulled over on an off ramp on Highway 16 near the Narrows Bridges and a State Patrol officer had the guy in the back of his car.

Driving away from there, Dean said, "Tacoma Police have a high speed chase ban. We can block the guy, but we can't chase him. If the guy would have got off the freeway and kept speeding, he might have gotten away. Let's get some lunch."

The majority of Tacoma's waterfront was known as Ruston Way. The jogging path along Ruston Way went from an old fishing wharf, down past a few restaurants, to the remnants of the

Asarco Smelter that had been closed down for twenty years. After stopping by a sandwich shop, we parked down near one of the restaurants and watched girls in small outfits jog by. Being a cop may not always be exciting, but unlike the security job, at least the scenery changed.

"So how long, have you and Lisa been together?"

"A little over a year. What about you? You married or something?"

"Yeah. Been married two years."

"She cool with you giving out your number to speeders?"

Dean smiled. "We have an arrangement."

"Okay."

"I take it you don't run around on Lisa?"

"No way."

"You should dude. You're young. A guy like you could do well."

Dean saw him before I did. He didn't say anything. He just dropped his sandwich and got out of the car. He left the car door open and ran towards a man with a Mohawk. He pulled his gun and started yelling something I couldn't hear. The guy stopped.

I heard Dean's cell go off in his seat. It was the standard text messaging tone. After a few moments, an automated voice read the message. "You. Are. So. Cute. Thanks. For. Dealing. With. Nick. I. Thought. He. Would. Find. Out. Everything."

I reached over and picked up the cell. I clicked through the previous text messages.

The first one being a little before midnight from Lisa's number:

Lisa: Stop by any time after six. Twenty ten Proctor. Apartment one.

The next one was shortly after Dean had picked me up that morning.

Dean: I thought he went 2 work at 6am. Not 6pm. Ride along was all I could think of.

I thought back on how he'd talked about his favorite things about his job was power and pussy. Something outside got my attention. Dean and the Mohawk guy were on the ground wrestling. I thought of something else Dean had said: "Shoot the fucker."

I flicked the switch, grabbed the shotgun and got out of the car. I pumped the shotgun. Mohawk had stood up and had Dean's gun. I stared at Dean.

The shotgun blast hit Mohawk in the shoulder. He fell, dropping the gun. Dean went to pick up the pistol. I pointed the shotgun at Dean. Dean gave me a look.

"Your wife called." I said, "She wants you to stop fucking my girlfriend."

I lowered the shotgun. Dean called it in.

An ambulance took the guy I shot to Tacoma General. We told our story a dozen times to half a dozen people. Then we wrote it down. Dean called the Food Mart and said I was helping with an investigation. Around midnight, we got to leave.

Dean and I were walking back to the car. We'd hardly said a word to each other.

"Let's get a beer." I said.

Dean looked at me.

"You want to have a beer with the guy who screwed your girlfriend?"

"I won't lie, Dean. I was pissed, but as I thought about everything that happened today, I realized something."

"What's that?"

"You never promised me anything. Lisa did. By sleeping with you, Lisa was being a slut. You though, you were just being a rock star."

Dean put on his sunglasses.

"You got that right, baby. Let's get drunk. I'm buying."

In Search of Richard Brautigan

David Fewster

"Is that you?"

asked the little 3rd grade girl

in the school playground where

I had taken my 2 year-old daughter.

She pointed to the cover of

Trout Fishing In America, which I was reading

While Hannah threw gravel at the monkey bars.

It must have been my hair

And the felt hat I was wearing.

"Yes," I replied.

"Yes, it is."

And went home famous.

***

I had my vasectomy done the weekend before I moved to Tacoma, which set the tone for the entire venture. Not to mention my entire life thereafter.

The topic of my vasectomy had been in the air for several months, the frequency and intensity of the conversations increasing after my wife's periods began after the birth of our daughter. To spare Hannah's feelings in the womb, I never referred to an "unplanned pregnancy", but rather to "our planned on a subliminal/subconscious level pregnancy." After a traumatic IUD experience, my wife had for the past decade relied on no birth control method other than an intimate knowledge of her life cycles. Amazingly, this method had only failed one other time, resulting in the birth five years previously of a son. The boy's father was born and raised in Rochester, New York, which was also the place of my birth and upbringing. I enjoyed pondering this fact like a dog worrying a chew toy, although I was never able to draw any solid conclusions from the coincidence.

Anyhow, two months after Hannah's arrival, menstruation commenced, which was quite disappointing because the doctor had implied a longer time frame before the danger of unprotected sex would rear its ugly head. Like most men, I was perturbed at the turn our birth control discussions seemed to have taken, feeling that my request that the matter be handled with a simple pill to be a reasonable alternative to irreversible martyrdom under the blade. To this line of discourse, however, I was treated to a veritable barrage straight from the Harvard Medical Journal regarding the chemical pillage inflicted on the female bio system by the pill, along with side arguments about world population and my faith in our long-term relationship. Finally, in January (by which time Hannah was four months old), I agreed to make an appointment at the Country Doctor, a sliding-scale clinic on Capitol Hill where I had once had my chronic eczema treated.

The first step was to take the pre-operative interview as required by state law. The doctor with the ponytail grimaced when he saw my scrotum.

"Hm, how long have you had this varicosity?" he asked, fingering my left testicle which, to the uninitiated, feels all the world like a myriad of copulating earthworms engaged in a primordial orgy. "Sometimes these veins get wrapped around the sperm duct and it's hard to tell what's what. If we can't find it, we'll have to call a specialist." Specialist? What's he trying to say? My dick is being sliced open by amateurs? What the hell am I doing in the Capitol Hill clinic anyway? If these freaks were so good, why aren't they working in real hospitals? I don't care if the Stranger ad did say they'd do the job for $10—it's all part of Dan Savage's sadistic plot against breeders. Visions of Dr. Benway dance in my head as I imagine the operating scene, the surgeon popping amyls and screaming "Nurse! I can't see worth shit through this muck—it's like a fucking rainforest in there"—while my cock, balls, appendix, and prostate gland are lopped off and thrown, sliding in bloody trails down office walls. "It's gotta be here somewhere…"

Winter passed into spring which passed into summer. Fights about my reticence regarding the slice-and-dice thing were interspersed with screams of rage regarding our landlords, the Blausteins. We were living in a nice neighbourhood in West Seattle in what was euphemistically called a "carriage house", i.e. a shack in the alley behind the main house where indentured servants from Sweden must have been herded like cattle a hundred years ago. 100 years was also the last time the roof on the death trap was patched, as evidenced by the rivulets of brown water that coursed down the walls into the electric socket by the baby's crib every time it rained more than two minutes. This, however, did not constitute an immediate hazard according to the county building inspector, who informed us my notion that water and electricity don't mix was unscientific superstition.

Our tragic, late-night demise from a fire started by a wiring short was miraculously averted, however, with the news of my wife's surprise inheritance from her recently-deceased step-grandmother, a woman she hadn't seen since the 70's. The 20 grand involved was our ticket out of Squalorville, the only question being "Where to?"

"Tacoma, of course," replied my wife. After the first wave of horror had passed, I realized there was a certain logic to this response. True, Tacoma was to Seattle what Oakland was to San Francisco, a crime-ridden cesspool whose gateway was a row of porn shops housed in crumbling brick ruins that hadn't seen better days since Coolidge was president. But, and this was a big 'but,' you could buy a house there for under $100,000. And, and this was a bigger 'and,' you could actually get owner-financing in the event you couldn't qualify for a bank loan. (And who the hell would live in Tacoma if they could qualify for a bank loan?) In fact, to the old codgers who owned the property my wife wanted to buy, my $22K job at a telecommunications firm made me the epitome of a white-collar career guy.

The drawback of the plan was the fear that if we missed a payment by a day we would, like the slaughterhouse worker in The Jungle, be thrown screaming into the gang ridden streets. On the other hand, there was the comforting knowledge that my wife's best friend Michelle lived there. They had met when Michelle was a wild hippie girl living on Vashon. Then, she moved to Bremerton to live with the co-owner of a tattoo parlour who cheated on her. Now she was married to a fellow who hooked up cable TV and owned a house on S. 17th and Prospect, which was far enough away from the Hilltop that you had to really strain your ears to actually hear the gunfire. The point was, things seemed to be looking up for Michelle, and there was no reason to believe that they wouldn't for us, too.

In the midst of the excitement of dealing with slumlords, realtors, and estate attorneys, however, the problem of my sterilization was not ignored. My wife, in an empathetic moment, sensed my squeamish attitude of having my scrotum slashed by a pimply-faced intern even if it did only cost the equivalent of a night out at Burger King, and went to the trouble to find the veritable Rolls-Royce dealership of vasectomy clinics. It was run by a legend, a man who was apparently the Einstein of gonad surgeons, a doctor so famous that other doctors had to take a course from him at the University of Washington just to be able to purchase the equipment used in his revolutionary new technique. My wife had generously (albeit not completely altruistically) offered to pay for this procedure, but it turned out my company insurance would cover it. (This created something of a personal milestone, as this was the first time I'd ever been able to combine a medical emergency with gainful employment.)

Unfortunately, this also entailed another series of "Why I Want a Vasectomy" interviews, the first with a bored GP in West Seattle who was required by my insurance provider as a referring physician, the second by the office manager at the clinic in University Village. While the intellectual part of these sessions was easy enough ("Yes, one child is enough for me, thank you, it'll be a goddamn miracle if I can keep her growing girlhood supplied with hot dogs and spaghetti-o's as it is without any further complications"), there was always that unvoiced, nagging doubt ("Gee, what if Winona Ryder wanted me to father her love child and then spurned me when she finds out I only shoot blanks…") The office manager turned out to be an attractive woman in her late forties, the only female bureaucrat I was required to tell my tale of woe. I scanned her eyes for a sympathetic reaction to my noble sacrifice, figuring my experience may make me one of those appealing, sensitive 90's guys that Cosmo is always telling us are hits with the babes.

Oddly enough, the question of potency didn't constitute one of my fears. I knew enough about the procedure to realize the likelihood of the entire works being chopped off was remote (particularly since my upgrade from the public health ghetto) and, not being Norman Mailer, the fact that the possibility of impregnation did not exist with every act of intercourse did not present a reason for the permanent abdication of my libido. And I never even attempted to use the line "Because I never expect to ever have a partner other than my wife for the rest of my life" in the fear that, after the laughter died down, my inquisitor would mark me ineligible for the operation due to reason of insanity. (Also, with one divorce each on our own scoreboards, our own marital record was not one to inspire confidence in most statisticians.)

At long last, the big day arrived. In a masterpiece of good life planning, I arranged for my vasectomy, a yard sale, and the packing, loading and transporting of all my worldly goods to an entirely different city to occur on the same weekend, so I wouldn't have tomiss any work. My first assignment, bright and early Saturday morning, was to skip breakfast (per orders) and get down to the clinic, where I would be the first customer of the day.

"Do you want to watch?" asked the Great Doctor, easer of pain for thousands of men a year. How could I refuse? And what kind of case would I have in a malpractice suit if I didn't, for that matter? As it turned out, I had nothing at all to worry about from that end-the entire operation was a veritable work of art performed by one who seemed more magician than scientist.

Instead of using two incisions, placed on either side of the scrotum just above where the sperm ducts meet the testes, Dr. Wilson does the just with just one, an incision so miniscule that it doesn't even require stitches. After injecting a shot of Novocain in my balls and waiting a couple minutes for it to take effect, he whipped out what looked like a tiny paper hole-puncher and punched a small hole in the middle of my scrotum. Taking out a thin, longish pair of tweezers, he reached through the hole, went down one side, and brought the tweezers back bearing what looked like the skinniest strand of angel hair pasta in the universe. Pulling out a good two inches of this fleshy filament, he cut a chunk off with a pair of scissors, cauterized the loose ends remaining with something out of an old wood-burning kit, and stuffed the mutilated works back into its sac faster than you could say "How in the love of Satan did he manage to find the right one so fast, what with all those other veins and tubes and shit down there?" The morning dew hadn't even dried from the parking lot when I got back in my car, bearing a plastic canister for a follow-up sample, a handful of Advil, and the admonitions to take it easy and not use my dick for anything fun for five days. In retrospect, I couldn't even remember seeing any blood.

My wife, not being quite sure how much the ordeal was going to take out of me, had arranged for me to spend a day at a cheap hotel where I could recuperate under more restful conditions than those provided by a yard sale presided over by an over-excited six-year old boy and his nine-month old sister. I helped move a couple of the heavier items out onto the cement driveway for the sale, and went in the house to lie down between the half-packed boxes until it was time to check in. The shot was starting to wear off, but the discomfort wasn't too extreme, not much worse than the feeling that lingers about an hour after you've been hit in the balls with a hockey stick. The plan was for me to hang out in the rented room until early evening, come back to West Seattle to help put away any unsold stuff, and drive the whole family back to the hotel for the night.

Out of a perverse nostalgia, I had decided to stay at the Thunderbird Hotel, a fleabag on Aurora Avenue in Fremont that had also been my accommodations on my very first visit to Seattle a decade before. Standing on the second-floor balcony, I smoked a cigarette and admired the view of the city as it loomed over the bridge, trying to remember which skyscrapers made their appearance after 1986 and wondering what would have been more unrecognizable—the present skyline or my new life? Tiring of profundity, I went inside and fell asleep over an old Dean Martin-Jerry Lewis movie. Ah, cable TV, once again your comforting bosom provides comfort from our afflictions.

Around six, I was tooling down 99 to pick up the clan. If anything, my nap had only made me groggy. The pain seemed about the same, although my mindset veered from its original clinical observation, which tended to be fascinated by the novelty of my new sensations, into a maudlin self-pity. Before we'd even pulled into the parking lot of the Thunderbird, I'd managed to get into a screaming argument with my wife. Maybe I thought she was being insufficiently grateful for the gift of my sterilization. Maybe I wanted Chinese take-out instead of pizza. Whatever the reason, it was enough to make me storm off and jump on a bus, black clouds of justified rage trailing behind me along with the exhaust fumes.

Hours later, I sat on the floor of the darkened, West Seattle house, pondering what my Existence had become. "My God, I'm the Anti-Matter Richard Brautigan!" I realized. charting the trajectory of my life, I found it ran in a mirror-image of the hippie novelist's, almost as if viewed from one of those alternative universes Stephen Hawking was always typing about. Instead of leaving a squalid Pacific Northwest and facing the pressures of being an unprepared family man in the big city only to emerge as the literary beacon of the post-beat generation, I was taking the entire trip backwards to end up in the very same Tacoma surroundings that informed Brautigan's ominous, early childhood memories in the stories from Revenge of the Lawn. The most noticeable difference being, of course, the 'literary beacon' analogy as applied to my own San Francisco years, where 'drunken little slacker poseur' would have been more accurate. Still, had not a poem of mine appeared in an obscure anthology alongside that of a certified Beat Legend who probably didn't get paid, either? Regardless of whatever might happen, they would never take that away from me and the theme music from "Gone With the Wind" blasted through my head as I curled up on an old laundry sack to sleep the good sleep of the Perfect Martyr.

Coda

Of course, my wife called then, we made up and I was back at the motel a mere six hours after my initial departure. I have blocked out the events of the subsequent days in all but a vague way, sort of like what happens to women after childbirth (because otherwise they would never go through the experience ever again and the human race would have died out in its earliest stage.) On my first trip with the moving van to the new house, however, I had a strange epiphany. Once, when I was a college student in upstate New York, I was walking one twilight through an older, residential neighbourhood between my campus and downtown Syracuse when I was gripped by the notion that if I kept on walking I would somehow be able to go back into time until I ended up at my grandparent's house on Bancroft Avenue. Driving over the ravine to the Sprague exit, I had the same feeling of being transported back to that tree-lined working-class suburb that had never left my three year-old psyche. The golden light from the setting sun gave the very soot an enchanted air, and our new street was lined with old-fashioned street lamps that must have dated from the turn of the century and were unceremoniously torn down a year after our arrival. That night, I tested my equipment to see if it still worked. It did.

The next morning, my wife and I dropped the dryer four feet off the back of the van, missing the ramp entirely and having the top come flying off like a defective jack-in-the-box. And, a few weeks later, I learned from the pages of the National Enquirer that Anthony Quinn, aged 81, had knocked up his secretary and was expecting his 687th illegitimate child, while Tony Randall, 77, was expecting his first.

Sometimes, the portents just come too fast to make any sense of them at all.

Deviant Light

Nick Stokes

They close the black door behind you. Across the room is a white door. The doors have no handles or knobs or buttons. Between you and the white door patients with shaved heads converse around round tables or gaze at mobile devices thrumming responsively to their touch or snack at the refreshment bar or do what normal people do. To the left is a window next to which nobody stands. To the right is a garish red stage curtain. Below the curtain the toes of a woman's pumps point toward a toilet base. The walls are off-white, the ceiling cream, the joints square. You finger the black box behind your right ear and trace the mole tunnels of diverging wires under your hairless scalp.

You know what has been done; you were told; you accepted the terms though your choices were terminal. Neural pleasure centres in your brain were infected with a virus that laced targeted cells with a photo-responsive protein. When the treated neurons are exposed to light, they are stimulated, releasing dopamine, creating pleasure. The progressive procedure positively reinforces good behaviour with the patient's own sense of gratification, satisfaction, and wellbeing instead of punishing retrograde behaviour with such costly techniques as financial sanction, coercion, incarceration, isolation, and euthanasia. The positive reinforcement procedure has proven more effective in laboratory trials than pharmaceuticals, psychological overhaul, and personality reboot. Through insignificant holes drilled in your skull a robotic arm threaded dozens of LEDs into your brain, aiming for the light-sensitive neural bundles. An electrode carrying neural signals out of your brain runs alongside each LED to communicate your mental performance, so that certain patterns of thought may be rewarded and you may be protected from such machinery malfunctions as brain overheating. The LED/electrode cables are four neurons thick. They were secured to small rigid polymer needles with a silk adhesive; the needles were implanted; the adhesive dissolved in your brain fluid; the polymer scaffolds were withdrawn. The cables remain. They attach to the black box behind your ear, which transmits your raw neural performance to a computer that evaluates the stream of information in a well-tested algorithm. The black box then receives signals to turn on the light in your dark brain when you perform a useful action or pursue optimism or accomplish an economically productive task or think well or don't shoot up or do something socially beneficial or in your case avoid your self-destructive cascade of deviance: sadness, futility, contrariness, hopelessness, apathy, pointlessness, depression, and defiance.

A thin bald woman creeps from behind the bathroom curtain into the light, wipes her mouth with a handkerchief she tucks into her rear jeans pocket, and walks deliberately to the refreshment bar, where a man shadowed with stubble holds a tumbler glass of brown liquid and stares into nothing. She takes a donut and sits at a vacant round table. You cross the room and pour yourself a cup of coffee. The white door opens and a clean-shaven burly young man in black interacting with the screen on his mobile device and acting no different than anyone else despite the gauge of the glow-in-the-dark blue flesh tunnels in his earlobes and the full-arm wing tattoos and the jagged repairable scar bisecting his face exits and the door shuts. The glass man does not acknowledge your proximity. You sit next to the donut woman, holding your coffee close. You who prefer to crawl into holes force yourself to say hello. Fellowship burns away your anxiety. She nods but says nothing. She eats her donut with determination. Your solidarity dims. Two wigged women holding hands and cooing bustle out the white door, which seems to open for them. The donut woman fidgets with her crumbs. You leave her and your coffee. You push on the white door; it is cold and solid and unresponsive. You make your way to the window. In a corner, a middle-aged man whose hair has grown back around his bald spot beats his head against the wall. The thud is rhythmic and smacks as it moistens. His forehead smears on the wall. He smiles, teeth turning red. A shaved child in a blue ball cap is led in through the black door. The nurses, one with a high blonde bun and one a long brunette braid, take the injured man under the armpits and he swoons. They drag him out the black door. Why, if he is happy and hurting nobody, you wonder, but you abandon your illogic. The bulb of an epiphany brightens without the comprehension. The glass man spins, rushes to throw back the red curtain, dumps his drink in the toilet, cries in relief, and falls to his knees, unable to stand the euphoria. Out the window below people stride here and there rectilinearly under full heads of hair and cars stop and go and a cacophony of pigeons swarms down from a gargoyle roost and dismantles a brownbag lunch dropped by a child in the shadow of a birch tree near a picnic bench where no vagrant sits or sleeps or mutters under a blue sky in which you cannot find the sun behind the skyscrapers so you jump in your mind's eye through the window, hurtling down among shards of glass, the world slowing or your consciousness expanding, the passers-by looking up at you in confusion as if entertaining the question for the first time, the birch leaves and papery bark peeled by some degenerate that is the only litter on the street coming into focus, the pigeons diving alongside you, cement approaching, but despite your gravity you swoop up in pursuit of the sun rising story-by-story past windows higher and higher and yes light shines on the flying you in your brain and the sun heats your face and you wrench yourself away from the window and slam shut your eyes to reclaim your vision and slam into concrete, darkness slamming into you, the rush and buzz and high ceasing abruptly, and the slight bounce of your body and the explosion of your brain and the spurt of your blood some distance onto your observers and the question of how long until you're forgotten and if anyone will care you're gone or if it matters. You shiver with cold sweats in the dark cavern behind your eyelids. You open your eyes, which require time to dilate. The glass man is pouring himself another drink. The donut woman trembles and sweats, like you, but she will not stand and go to the toilet, she will not go behind the curtain, she will not. Making the rounds, a frail young red-rimmed woman with a flat discontinuity on the right side of her cranium approaches you and says, "Hello, how are you, fine, thanks," and moves on to the next person. You wonder if you received credit for the flying despite the self-death scenario. The glass man takes his drink to the toilet, dumps it, falls to his knees. The donut woman, rigid, straight-backed, hands clutching her seat, vomits on the table and then gasps breath. The vomit smells sour with an undercurrent of sweet. Her face relaxes, softens, brightens. Why fight? Why not be how you should be. You imagine curling up in the darkest corner and crying, or not crying. It doesn't matter. An abyss fills your skull; electrodes conduct you out drill holes. You coil there for days, reveling in uselessness, perseverating on meaninglessness, resisting non-violently, not fighting, cooperating, docile, until you are too hungry. You feel the ecstatic blaze when you surrender to thoughtlessness and stand to swill apple juice and wolf a bagel smothered in cream cheese from the refreshment bar and you imagine a scenario in which you get a steady data management job and propose to the evacuated woman and make enough money to spend -- white ignites and your legs buckle but you won't but you can't think under the interrogation light threatening to so completely consume the darkness that it becomes darkness. You cling to a hollow of nothing within, a grounding point in the lifting expansion of light, a solid form in the wash of dark, and take pleasure in the pleasure dimming, in having scarcely held onto yourself while with your mind you induced a doctored hit. You do not curl up in the corner. With unnecessary force you thump a stack of brown paper towels on the donut woman's slop and wipe up thin bile thick with donut as slow as you can, understanding, lingering with the smell. Enlightenment dawns in your brain, but you defy their satisfaction by swallowing a chunk of her stinking vomited donut and create your own by relishing the unsanitariness of your cleansing and the imagined stupefaction of your observers. The donut woman steps in to hug you but you kiss her filthy mouth hard and then push her flushing face away without further response. People surround you in the room doing what people do. Nothing. The glass man, able again to stand, totters to the refreshment table, shakily pours himself a drink, sloshes on his way to the toilet, dumps it in while clinging to the red curtain for support, and falls to his knees. You close your eyes to better be the bloom of the stolen kiss in the dark your brain illuminates.

Covert Operation Calico

L. Lisa Lawrence

The story you are about to hear is true.

Only the names have been changed to protect the innocent.

Since no one was actually innocent, I didn't bother.

There are friends you call in the dark of the night, when you need someone to help move furniture. That was my friend Houston S Wimberly the Third.

There are friends you call in the dark of the night, when you need to move a body... Apparently, that would be me.

When Houston called late one night, distraught after finding his dear sweet kitty, Callie the Calico laying lifeless on the chair she had been napping on earlier that afternoon, I instructed him to wrap her up and put her in the freezer until we could come up with a plan. It wasn't the most dignified thing to do, but it served two purposes. To put her and his guilt for carelessly throwing his jacket onto the chair she was on and not noticing her out of his sight, and to keep her body from starting to smell in the summer heat of his non air conditioned third floor apartment.

The next day, when we were both rested and had time to think, we discussed ideas for her final resting place. Both of us being artists, meant that those ideas were going to be... uh... creative.

OK, some of them were flat out weird. Initially, he wanted to try to bury her in Wright Park, a one hundred year old arboretum in the heart of the city. Don't get me wrong, it would have been a great place. Guarded by two goddesses to the North and two lions to the South, the park is home to an amazing collection of trees and flowers, a beautiful conservatory, our winter sledding hill and a then headless statue in the pond we liked to refer to as "The Lady of the Lake".

There was no place in Tacoma quite as cool as Wright Park. Of course, that location was not without challenges. During the day, crowds were there enjoying the paths, playground and the slimy wading pool. In addition to the human crowds, were the "Urban Commando Squirrels From Hell", cheeky, fearless little creatures that looked cute, but were in all actuality, a highly organized crime ring. Roaming the park in packs, they would strategically place themselves in the middle of the trails to stop walkers and stare them down with an unspoken, yet very clearly delivered, "Gimme' yer nuts and no-one gets hurt".

At night, a different, more nefarious crowd took over the park, lurking in the shadows of the dark central area out of sight of the surrounding streets and neighbourhood. It was not a place you went at night to commit a low level criminal act. This was no place for amateurs.

Once I convinced him of the impossibility of getting away with burying a dead frozen cat in one of the highest traffic areas in the city (never mind us here with the shovels, we're not doing anything creepy at all), we came up with a more fitting location for Callie's last resting place. It was still a bit risky, because there had to be laws about where one can bury a dead cat.

I was willing to bend a few rules neither of us were clear on in order to help a friend honor the life and passing of his beloved fur child. It certainly wasn't going to harm anyone, so we came up with another location in the area of a nameless park, with a nameless zoo, next to a nameless body of water. It was perfect

Neither one of our employers would have looked kindly on us if we had been arrested while sneaking around with a shovel and a body, so we had to make sure we pulled this off undetected.

And so, with the help of a third co-conspirator, "Covert Operation Calico" was born.

When I go covert, I go covert, and planned down to the last detail, including what to do and say in every possible worst case scenario. Callie was getting a respectful and sacred burial.

The more serious I got about pulling this off, the more hilarious my friends thought my stories and planning were and the goofier they got.

I had advised them that since this was a covert operation, that we would need collapsible shovels or spades that could be concealed our day packs, and at least one pack large enough for kitty, who needed to be wrapped up so as not to draw attention to the fact that we were hauling around a dead frozen cat.

I had several stories ready to give the authorities in the event that we were stopped or questioned. The first story would be that we were out hunting for (out of season) Chanterelle mushrooms or geocaching. The stories would become more elaborate as we got further into the operation.

We parked far enough away from the crowds that we could get the cat out of the box and into the pack. This is when the first logistical challenge made itself known. In his grieving state, Houston hadn't wrapped Callie up in a towel or t-shirt to put her in the freezer, he had wrapped her in a very thick bathroom rug which was now frozen to her stiff body. He must have had one big freezer.

We decided against taking the heavily used wooded trail, and instead chose to take the shoreline from an unnamed beach to an area that is difficult to get to and not heavily travelled, especially when it is raining, the tide is rising and the sun is going down.

The cat would not fit in the backpack due to the large rug she was wrapped in and the odd angles her stiff legs jutted out of said rug. Seriously, how did all of this fit in his freezer?

We walked down the beach as casually as we could, I with a frozen dead cat hanging out of my day pack, with Houston walking behind me making sure that the body didn't fall out pretending that we were going out for a picnic. Morgain had her bright orange backpacking "poop trowel" in the side of her back, like a beacon saying, "Hey look at us!" At that point, our cover story changed to, we were going out for a sunset picnic which we over packed for, and Morgain has to poop a lot.

We were like three naughty kids out on an unapproved adventure giggling at the absurdity of it all. Of course, we started laughing hysterically which did not help us avoid drawing attention to our allegedly covert activities.

Things got complicated when we reached our destination. Some local teenagers had chosen the same isolated area to smoke pot. They didn't want to light up in front of the old folks who could be narcs, and we didn't want to bury a body (even if it was feline) in front of any witnesses; so both groups stood there staring at each other, reminiscent of a scene from "The Good The Bad And The Ugly".

We didn't have time for this foolishness; the sun was going down and the tide was coming in. We had no intention of needing rescue and being on the evening news.

Finally, after what seemed like an eternity, the kids, apparently disgusted by the turn of events wandered off down the beach and we were able to explore our options away from their prying, judging, bloodshot eyes.

I had a story prepared if we were caught with the dead cat at this stage of the operation, but it was a good one, and I'm going to save it, in case I ever need to use it again.

After searching up and down the beach and bluff, we decided on what we could only describe as a "natural cathedral" overlooking the water. The digging wasn't easy considering the tools we brought had to fit in our day packs and Morgain's bright plastic poop trowel certainly wasn't designed to chip away at clay. We managed to dig a proper sized hole and release the now partially thawed Callie from her blanket.

The three of us solemnly laid Houstons' beloved fur child to rest in her cathedral with the beautiful view of the setting sun, sang "Amazing Grace" (despite the fact that we were all certified heathens) and spoke a blessing. We then sat there in silence contemplating life, death and friendship until the incoming tide began lapping at our feet.

As we began the long trek back to the parking area, we commented on what a beautiful little ceremony it was and that anyone, human or fur child would be lucky to have one like it.

Rest in Peace Callie.

Rest In Peace Houston

4/5/1951 – 3/29/2012

Geography

Michael Haeflinger

What I didn't know made sense.
Like I didn't know that the sun
was made of wicker, or people
sometimes have eyes embedded
in the small of their backs.
That's the eastside, like
that one time I stopped
for spinach pie at the only
halal deli in town
and it had too much vinegar.
Down the road from there
was that Taco Bell
and its parking lot
full of regrets
and how the 2 a.m. line
would bend out onto Wayne Ave.
and how we'd stumble in full
of Wild Turkey and smoke a bowl

while watching late night cartoons.

I also didn't know that the river

was mostly drinking itself,

mostly its own veins emptied

along the silt of its skeleton.

So many afternoons

along the goose turd highway.

She had this look like,

you need to get out of this room

before you say something

really stupid. That was the northside:

all those tired strip clubs

and pancake houses,

all those hashbrowns

drowning in butter.

When her dad died, she waited

at the gates of the cemetery

for his resurrection.

In the middle

of the third night,

she awoke from a dream

about turtles carrying inchworms

in tiny pouches tied to their legs

and she walked home

through the neighborhoods

full of blacks

and old jewellery stores

that had been converted

into hair extension shops

and check cashing joints.

That was the west side.

That wasn't really the west side,
but that was what we thought
when we thought west side.
We never really went there.
Except for those few months
I delivered pizzas
on the west side and there was a porch
full of blacks
and I approached
and the woman came out
and said, don't be scared, nobody is going to rob you
and she didn't say ain't no one gon' rob you
and she didn't say boy, ain't no one gon' jack yo' shit
and she gave me a check and a cash tip
and took my empty pizza bag out to the car
limp and hanging over my arm like triage
or like washroom attendant or like maître d.
That west side was full of speed bumps and gates.

After work, I'd go back to the east side
and after that, I'd go someplace else,
I forget now where. The south side
was a razor blade for a city full of angels.

I never went to the south side.

Matterhorn

Titus Burley

Screams from inside the mountain. Distorted in pitch because of the speed with which they moved. Grimacing faces flashing in and out of view as the carts of death careened along a doomed circuitous track. A passage of courage or some collective form of voluntary madness? The unearthly wails from within suggested the latter.

Surrounding him, looming monstrous, were stinky bodies scorched red by the afternoon sun. Glistening visages and limbs slick with sweat, stifling in their proximity, moving in a slow, forward shuffle, dragging him along with them like some unrelenting human riptide.

Mortality. Inevitable death. Numbered breaths. Panic set his heart to pounding like a rabbit cornered by a slavering beast. Was there not some way to escape? Ten years old. A boy. So young to die.

When had meekly giving in become valor? Wasn't it better to bolt? To claw one's way out of the queue and run? To throw one's shoulder against the mighty tide and break free? Centuries of victims - from the drugged to the sober - accepted the rope, bowed before the guillotine, obligingly boarded the death train.

30 Minutes From This Point declared the sign. A countdown of minutes that would become seconds. He fought back the tears, refusing to cry. No one else would understand this courage. No one but God… if God were watching and listening that is. So many people in this line, hundreds, and in the surrounding acres, thousands, and in the city, millions, and in the world, billions. Why would

God amidst the ceaseless pangs of earth hear his particular cry for help?

Faith. The faith of a mustard seed. Faith that would move mountains, or completely *remove* them. Daniel in the lion's den. Shadrack, Meshack, and Abednego in the fiery furnace. If it be thy will, let this cup pass from me.

His brother was to blame. Richard. That bastard. Michael didn't know the meaning of the word but his brother spat it like a curse whenever someone angered him or created an obstacle to victory. And Richard, at thirteen, was all about winning, about asserting his will and getting his way. "Competitive," his parents had always said of his older brother with a chuckle. Blinders they wore; laughing away a character trait that would lead to the torment of others - himself in particular.

The mountain had of course been Richard's idea - his obsession for weeks. And not for himself, but a vicarious compulsion exclusively focused on Michael. "We'll make a man out of you yet, chicken." Great. This coming from a guy who thought it knee-slappingly funny the day before an airplane flight to Acapulco to predict during a game of Yahtzee that if Michael rolled three sixes - exactly what he needed on his last frame to make top and get the 35 point bonus - that their plane would crash. What lurked in the heart of someone to say something so twisted? When the trio of sixes had tumbled out of the shaker cup Michael had flung the plastic cup at his brother's head in point blank rage understanding in that precise moment why Cain slew Abel. Only siblings could generate a fury that defied reason. So he had won the battle but lost the war. He had prevailed in Yahtzee but was so torn up by fear that even touching down crash free in Acapulco could not allow him to fully enjoy the dream family vacation. For there remained a return flight that the dice had predicted he would not survive.

Yet he had survived and a year later Richard's mission to "toughen you up and get you to be less of wuss" had led to another vacation horror. They had split off from their parents an hour ago with an agreement to meet in front of The Golden Horse Shoe Revue at 1 p.m. for lunch. Like that would happen. He could see the park personnel presenting his mangled carcass to his parents, pulling back the sheet to verify identity. Dental records would no doubt be required for certainty.

Richard would probably survive with minor injuries. Even at ten, the inequities and unfairness of life rang loud and clear in Michael's ears - and perversely, like some mad banshee raving, that unfairness found its soundtrack in the screams which loomed closer with every step. The zigzag forward movement of the queue took them out of the sun and into a tunnel, a claustrophobic cavern that appeared to be hewn out of real stone. But how could that be? For this mountain was a manmade construction, one that until ten years before had not even existed.

Another sign estimated only ten more minutes of wait time. Could it really be that those around him grew giddy? Gleeful in their anticipation? It defied logic that people paid money for this. Intentionally chose this fate. Why would anyone except for a noble cause volunteer for agony and pain?

To cope, Michael focused on miracles. They happened. Like those astronauts who went to the moon. Surely they expected to die. Even at their most stout hearted moment, a niggling fear of obliteration must have tugged at the corners of courage. Yet somehow they returned intact. Heroes. Men of incredible valor.

"I will go out like an astronaut," Michael decided. Live or die, he would screw his courage to the sticking post as he had heard someone once say on TV and even if he had to close his eyes tight and grip the handrails until his knuckles turned white, he would meet this executioner.

"Scared?" asked Richard, nudging him. "You look like you're about to barf."

"I'm fine," Michael muttered.

"Don't embarrass me ever again like you did with the height requirement sign."

Michael had tried to slump down enough that his head would not reach the marker, but the teen working the line who had been dressed like one of the Von Trapp kids on a picnic with Maria in *The Sound Of Music* told him to "Stand up straight, kid." Thus achieving the height requirement, he had sealed his fate and likely signed his death warrant.

"And don't even think about changing your mind," continued Richard. "People younger than you do this all the time. It's time to stop being a sissy and be a man."

"Can't you just be quiet until it's over?" Michael blurted.

"Sure. Just don't crap your pants. You do that and I'll disown you as a brother."

And so the forward march of progress, the inevitable trickle of the sands of time, the one step after another process of movement brought them to the Matterhorn Mountain loading dock. Four people who had survived the experience removed themselves from the bobsled and stepped rather shakily toward the exit. Michael and Richard and two strangers - a shaggy haired youth and his pixie haired girlfriend who had anonymously shadowed the siblings during the forty minute wait for this moment - were buckled securely into the bobsled by another Von Trapp family looking Disneyland employee.

"No turning back now," said Richard, flashing what Michael had always considered his brother's version of an *evil grin*.

Michael swallowed back the bile rising in his throat and closed his eyes tightly as the sickening grind of gears caught their bobsled in its grip and began carrying them upward to the point where they would be released into a twisting, topsy-turvy, plummet into a sure abyss.

Happiest place on earth?

Not at that moment.

Janie's Got A Car

Karen Harris Tully

I scowled into my rearview mirror at the guy behind me next to the Suburban, threw my arm over the passenger seat of my new-to-me Sentra, and looked over my shoulder. My foot hovered over the accelerator. The shrinks had given me the labels of depression, anxiety, PTSD, survivor's guilt… sex addict… it just depended on which one you talked to. None of them, however, had tagged me as homicidal. Boy, somebody had sure missed something.

5 months earlier-

"Come on, Janie, hurry it up! Ash will be here any minute!" Terrell parked his vintage Trans-Am and turned off the radio along with the engine. He carefully scooped up his perfect girlfriend's miraculously intact cake from its perch on the front seat and hurried into the Dairy Royale without waiting for me.

What a douche. I swear, football stars. All that creatine must go to their heads. I once again turned myself into a pretzel in his miniscule backseat to pull my favorite red cowboy boots back on, still singing the song he'd turned off. Psycho Killer by the Talking Heads. I wish I'd destroyed that damn cake when I had the chance.

It was Princess Ashley's favorite for some unknown reason, strawberry swirl rainbow chip from the bakery 45 minutes away, with the photo of her as Fair Queen last summer. Terrell loved that photo of her. Terrell loved her. Or so he claimed when he wasn't busy screwing other girls.

"I'm coming, I'm coming. Sheesh!" I grumbled to myself and squirmed out of the back seat with a somewhat squashed tissue-froufed gift bag and one drive-thru drink cup of incriminating evidence. Why did I always get stuck with clean-up duty? I considered leaving the cup for Terrell to deal with, or briefly, dropping it into the gift bag as an added surprise for Ashley. But no, that would be rude even for me, and I liked my arrangement with Terrell the way it was.

So I threw the cup in the trash and went inside, ready to play nice girl next door again. On the plus side, food was on the house 'cuz Ashley's parents owned the Dairy Royale, and Shelly the manager overlooked Terrell's completely redundant cake. As usual, no one paid attention to me arriving with the birthday-girl's boyfriend. They all knew we were neighbors out in the sticks and I was always bumming rides. No big.

"OMG, they are nauseating together!" my best friend Bev exclaimed awhile later as we escaped into the momentarily-empty ladies room to touch up our makeup and chat. Off-key strains of Happy Birthday filtered in through the door from Ashley's throng of adoring fans. Gag me.

Bev and I had escaped to park ourselves in front of the large island of sinks and mirrors at the center of the newly remodeled bathroom. Faux-marble stalls lined the perimeter and one of those air freshener thingies on the wall spritzed tropical scent at us every few minutes.

"No kidding, right?" I rolled my eyes. "Do you ever wonder if Ash would be half as popular if her parents didn't own half the town?" She snorted at me.

"Are you forgetting that she's also sweet, beautiful, and kind to animals?" she asked.

"Don't forget dumb as a post," I muttered.

"And that's the only reason you and Terrell have gotten away with messing around behind her back for so long. You keep it up and it's gonna come back to bite you."

"I'm not trying to steal him away or anything, Bev. I'm just borrowing him once in a while," I mock-pouted. She laughed and shook her head at me.

"Can't you 'borrow' someone else?"

"I've tried," I whined pathetically at her, only half joking. "But you know how boys talk. I've got a couple of guys on tap when I'm out of town, but Terrell's the only one I know around here who can keep his mouth shut. Besides, you know what they say about black guys right?" She huffed and rolled her eyes. "Well, it's true." I pointed my eyeliner at her in the mirror.

"God, I can't wait till we graduate and can get out of this podunk town," I complained. 17 years had been long enough.

The door to the corner handicapped stall caught my attention in the mirror as it swung slowly open behind us. Surprising, because we'd checked under all the stalls when we came in and hadn't seen any feet. I was sure no one else was in here. Bev and I paused, both of us staring at the mirror, waiting for someone to come out. Oh, crap. Whoever it was had heard our whole conversation. When no one appeared after several seconds we both turned and ducked to look under the row of stalls again. Still nothing. We turned back to exchange a look in the mirror that said, WTF?

"Ok, weird," I said. "It's the haunted bathroom stall, dun, dun, dun," I intoned.

"No kidding, right? Bizarro." We both laughed and turned back to the mirror.

"Ok, what is your trick with eyeliner? I can never get mine…" I was staring intently at her eyes when they suddenly rounded like an anime character's in the mirror. My eyes followed hers to a man now leaning in the doorway to the handicapped stall. He was grinning creepily at us and buttoning his jeans with one hand. He must have been either standing on the toilet seat or sitting with his feet up. I did not want to know what he'd been doing in there.

"Ew!" Bev dropped her expensive kabuki brush into the sink, but managing to hold onto her even more expensive powder blush.

"Dude, Are you drunk? You're in the women's bathroom." Just looking at him, I pegged him for a logger. We had plenty of those around here, some of whom you could expect to be drunk any given night after work. He wore typical logger gear: double-front Carharts, striped hickory shirt, suspenders, and ugly-as-sin, slip-on Romeos. He was leaning against the stall doorjamb and held something casually behind the faux marble wall that I would have bet was a six-pack of Busch tallboys with at least five missing.

His smile changed to a glower and his eyes glittered with menace as he finished buttoning his pants and pulled his other arm out from the stall. The glint of silver, I was expecting, but not shape of the small Stihl chainsaw. So much for tallboys.

Bev screamed and I froze. "Buddy, what are you doing," I asked warily. He grinned again, raised it up over his head and ripped the cord. The roar of the chainsaw echoed around the tiled room.

"Run!" I yelled at Bev. We ran toward the door but realized we wouldn't get there with enough time to open the inward-swinging door. We ran around the island of sinks with him clomping after us in those ugly ass Romeos. We were on the opposite side of the island when he swung the roaring chainsaw into the mirrors between us with a deafening crash. Glass showered us as we cringed against the door, covering our heads. When I looked up again, he was climbing over the island countertop toward us. I grabbed the blush, still open and forgotten in Bev's hand, and hurled the whole thing at his grinning face. It hit with a puff of Petal Pink Shimmer that blossomed into a sparkly pink cloud around his head. The chainsaw sputtered out as he lost his grip on the trigger, waving a hand in front of his face and coughing.

"Go! Go!" I yanked the door open, shoved Bev out and ran while he was distracted.

Bev and I ran screaming down the hall back into the restaurant and toward the nearby exit. We shoved past Shelly, the irate manager, who was hurrying to find out what the roaring and crashing noises were coming from her new bathroom.

"No! Run!" I yelled back at her, but she didn't stop, straight-arming her way through the bathroom door just as the guy with the chainsaw started it back up again. Her brief scream was cut off abruptly and the sound of the chainsaw changed to a horribly lower, labored pitch for a few moments before returning to its former high wail.

The people in the busy restaurant were mostly staring in shock. Some of them were standing and gaping uncomprehendingly at the roaring noise of a chainsaw inside the Dairy Royale, but they were not yet moving. The exit was right in front of us, but the line from the counter blocked it with kids waiting to order on someone else's tab. Why was there only one exit in this place?

"Move! Move! Get out!" I tried to push my way through the crowd with Bev at my heels. They saw the guy coming down the hall after us and panicked, pushing and shoving, jamming people into the doorway. I realized we were trapped and not knowing what else to do, ran around the corner and into the restaurant, losing track of Bev.

The people stuck in the doorway were sitting ducks when chainsaw guy got to them. He quickly swung his weapon through the crowd at chest height, opening up a bloody line across the screaming mass of people and effectively stuffing the doorway with moaning, writhing bodies.

Not even pausing, the guy roared and swung the chainsaw around the corner after me, shredding the 8-foot plastic ice cream bar that had stood there as long as I could remember. Mr. Dip's smile shot a three foot arc of sparks that illuminated chainsaw guy's sparkly face and shirtfront.

Snuffy, a fat redneck nicknamed for the perpetual wad of Copenhagen in his lower lip, stood and pulled a handgun from his extended waistband and aimed it right over my shoulder. I dove out of the way under a booth as the gun went off, missing widely as Snuff was jolted by the panicking mob. Plaster rained down over the dining room.

Our would-be savior was buffeted on all sides by people running and screaming around him as chainsaw guy advanced, grinning manically and swinging the chainsaw back and forth through anyone and everything he could reach, blocking the kitchen. Blood and guts spattered nearby tables and Snuff shot several more times, hitting the soft serve maker and exploding the waffle cone display before he finally got a shot close. Unfortunately, it pinged off the whirling chainsaw blade and through the head of a really annoying know-it-all from my chem class, spraying gray matter on a flock of cheerleaders running past. When she said she wanted to share her brain with those less fortunate, I don't think that was what she meant.

People desperate to escape threw chairs through plate glass windows, showering me with glass in my hiding spot and trapping me under the booth as they scrambled over my table to safety. Across the room, I saw a dumpy, middle-aged worker lose her mind completely and get stuck trying to dive headset-first through the drive-thru window.

The roar of the chainsaw was so close now as I cowered under that booth, trying to make myself invisible in the corner. Snuffy's legs backed toward me as he fired his last shot and tried to run. My booth shook as he scrambled onto one seat and tried to go over the table and out the window. His high-pitched scream above me as the chainsaw found him made me clap my hands over my ears against the painful sound.

The whole booth jolted around me and a waterfall of hot blood cascaded over the table edge onto my shoulder a second before his heavy body fell onto the seat right next to my head, his dying eyes finding mine for his last moments. The table vibrated and shook above me as the chainsaw cut into it. That's it, it's all over, I thought. This redneck's dead fish eyes are the last thing I'm going to see. No, I corrected, his chew spit dribbling onto my leg is the last thing.

Suddenly I heard sirens. They chainsaw stopped. Psycho hopped up onto the other booth seat and out the window into the night. A golf ball-sized wad of chew rolled out of Snuffy's mouth and landed with a splat on my red cowboy boot. I rolled over and puked my guts out.

Later, I sat in the parking lot with a blanket wrapped around me, staring in confusion at a cup of hot coffee that had found its way into my hand. I don't drink coffee.

I'd been checked out by the EMTs and my dad was there to take me home, looking angry and lost a few feet away as I gave my statement to the police. He would handle this like anything else since Mom ran off with the local male stripper, with silence and a fifth of his old friend Jack.

TV crews from the big city showed up, but the reporters were all held behind a line of yellow police tape, able only to impotently yell questions and shove a microphone at anyone who passed close enough. At some point, the police chief gave a statement.

Some of the people made it out ok through windows, a few through the kitchen. Terrell and Ashley had ironically hidden in the bathroom. In all the running and people jumping into cars and scattering, the psycho with the chainsaw had disappeared. Poof, like smoke. As if I'd only imagined him. But I didn't imagine Bev lying amongst the black plastic-wrapped bodies in the parking lot.

***

Months later, things were starting to get – well, back to normal wasn't right. Some days I didn't think things would ever be normal again. I'd been through a ream of therapists and they had all sorts of names for it. Whatever. I should have been the one, not Bev, not all those people standing in the doorway just waiting for ice cream. Terrell's condom clothed dick now functioned as escapism.

The funerals were over, thank God. Time to get back to the business of living, that's what people said. So, I went through the motions of finishing out the school year. Graduation was just one more memorial service.

The school helped me line up a summer internship at the bank and I was saving my money to get out of this hell-hole of a town. One day near the end of June, I squashed myself into a corner of the bank's drive-up window to count change because the ancient coin machine had died, again. My co-worker Theresa came up beside me.

"Janie, you've got a visitor," she smiled at me. She was a kindly, middle-aged lady who'd taken me under her wing, reminding me to eat lunch and take breaks. I looked over to see Pretty Princess Barbie Ashley, standing at the counter, grinning at me as if we were best friends. She waived a book over her head.

"Janie, Janie! Our senior annuals finally arrived!" she said, loud enough for the whole bank to hear. Ms. Mitchell, the bitchy assistant manager just glared at me from her desk and tapped her watch to let me know she was timing my break. Ashley made it a habit to come by the bank a couple times a week to chat.

Her scrawny bird arm emphasized how skinny she'd gotten since the attack, but unlike me, she'd just bought a whole new size 0 designer wardrobe. I was sure I looked like her poor scarecrow cousin in my thrift store business outfit as she fake smooched my cheeks.

"Hi Ash," I forced a smile. Her dad, "Big" Earl Dixon, owned the bank and I had to stay on his good side. Which meant being nice to Ashley. The staff didn't call him the Earl of Dickdom for nothing.

Everyone hated his guts, especially Ms. Bitchell who was always worse when he was around. Usually Big Earl left the day-to-day running of the bank to the manager, but she was out at a conference that day so he was 'filling in'. Also known as making our lives hell.

"That's really nice of you, but I didn't buy an annual," I told her. Too many memories of friends who weren't here anymore. They were late because of all the changes that had had to be made.

The school should have just cancelled them.

"I know, I was on the committee. But," she lowered her voice to a whisper that somehow still carried, "I knew that was just because you couldn't afford it, so I bought you one!"

"Well, gosh Ashley, thank you," I replied. She didn't seem to catch the thinly veiled sarcasm in my voice. She pushed the book toward me, back cover up. Some loser brainiac at school thought Psycho Killer by the Talking Heads was appropriate for our class song. The same song that had been playing on the radio right before the massacre. Dark humor is apparently a coping mechanism.

"Hey, did you get a call from that TV producer who wants to do a special on the Chainsaw Killer?" Ashley asked. I grimaced at the name the TV stations had given him after the attack. Totally lame, IMO. There were reward and wanted posters up all around the country with his grainy picture from a security camera next to the artist's sketch from my description. His face in the bathroom mirror was still burned into my memory.

"He said it would be very high-brow," she continued. "I gave him your numbers. Maybe it'll help them catch the guy." She seemed optimistic, but really, none of it helped. He was just so average. None of the logging companies recognized him and in the rural northwest, everyone and their brother owned a chainsaw. Some people thought he must have spent some time here, had something against the town, but no one knew him.

"No. Actually, I don't have a cell anymore." Someone kept giving my number to every TV station and newspaper in the country. "And my dad hangs up on those people."

"O.M.G! That must be terrible! How do you live without a cell phone? You poor thing!" she exclaimed so loudly that everyone in the bank looked our way. She dug around in her purse, not noticing the attention she'd brought us, and pulled out a business card.

"Here, you should call him," she put the card on top of the year book and pushed them both toward me. "We can do the show together, it'll be fun!" Her eyes glittered maniacally and I wondered, not for the first time, if Ashley was really all there anymore.

"No. Thank you, but that would really not be fun for me," I replied.

"Oh." She pouted. "Well, keep the card and think about it, ok?" I nodded and she beamed as if I'd just told her yes. I'd think about it all right, that very evening while I lit the card on fire and used it as kindling to burn the yearbook.

"Oooh, look at the time," she looked at her cell. "I've got to get going or I'll be late for my massage." As if on cue, her father stepped out of the manager's office.

"Ashley, I'd like to speak to you for a moment," Big Earl boomed across the bank. No one in that family knew how to be quiet.

"But Daddy, I…"

"No buts, Ashley. Get in here."

"O-kay," she glanced longingly at her brand-new gold Lexus, visible through the front window because she'd parked in the handicapped stall. She trudged into the office, leaving the door ajar.

I went back to my menial task at the drive-up counter and tried to seem like I wasn't listening to Big Earl interrogate Ashley about why she hadn't been wearing the diamond encrusted Rolex her parents had given her for graduation. I shook my head and looked out the window. It goes with everything! I recalled Ashley gushing.

The drive-thru was at the back of the building, facing a forested hillside and with a view of the dumpster at the back of the parking lot. A big rig had been parked there all morning. Probably a long haul trucker catching some sleep. I watched as a man in a plaid shirt, suspenders, and Romeos hopped out of the cab and into the parking lot. He glanced over at me and our eyes locked for a moment before he walked out onto the sidewalk toward town. He whistled, with his hands in his pockets, his sandy-brown hair blowing in the early summer breeze.

"Janie? Janie what is it?" Theresa asked. She crouched down next to me and I realized I was now kneeling on the floor, peering over the counter at the man walking down the street.

"Th-that's him," I stammered, pointing over the counter. "Theresa, that's him," I repeated.

She got all wide-eyed. "Are-are you sure?" she whispered. I began to have doubts. There were plenty of men who matched his description, plenty of average men with shaggy, light-brown hair and logger clothes.

"I'm sure," I heard myself say. We called the police and found out they were all out on a call, but the dispatcher promised they would track the man down as soon as possible. I don't think she believed me though, that it was Psycho Killer just out for a stroll down the street. I think the police had been called out for every brown haired logger in the county in the past months.

God, why hadn't I gotten a handgun? I'd thought about it, but I was too young for a concealed weapons permit and my dad was worried I might do something stupid. Besides, it hadn't worked for Snuffy, and I hadn't wanted the idiots at school singing "Janie's Got a Gun" at me all the time. Terrell. Terrell carried a gun now. But I'd given up my cell phone to save money, damn it!

A short while later, I saw the man walk back with a plastic sack from the mini-mart. Maybe it wasn't the same guy. Maybe he would just leave. Please just leave.

As he climbed into the cab of his truck, there were still no police to be seen. I let out the breath I hadn't realized I was holding when he pulled the truck around and pointed it toward the exit. But my relief was premature. He opened his door and climbed out again. He left the truck running and reached back in for the Stihl.

"Lock the doors! Call 911!" I yelled in a panic. Theresa and I ran around locking all the bank doors while everyone else was pretty much frozen in a state of shock. Someone frantically called 911 again while a few others got in gear and ran around pulling the window shades. Ashley and her father came running out of the office.

"Young lady!" Big Earl thundered. Ms. Bitchell cowered at her desk. "What do you…." He spotted Psycho out the backdoor window with his chainsaw and just stood there, his jaw flapping like a fish.

As soon as the last door was locked, I dove for a desk phone and quickly dialed the number of my favorite booty call.

"Ter, he's here!" I shouted when he answered. "He's here at the bank Ter."

Ashley stood next to her father, moaning and swaying. "No, no! What is he doing here? He's not supposed to be here." Her little clutch purse fell to the marble floor with a heavy thunk.

Ms. Bitchell panicked and ran into the vault, locking herself inside. Big Earl strode over and started pounding on the thick steel door, leaving Ashley to slide to the floor in a designer puddle. He stopped pounding for a second, swearing and searched his pockets. He swore again and resumed pounding on the door. Great, the owner of the bank didn't even have the vault combination.

With the bank manager gone, the rest of us were locked out of the reinforced steel room. The Earl of Dickdom continued pounding on the door and yelling at Bitchell as Psycho Killer outside ripped his chainsaw to life and went for the locked backdoor.

"We've gotta get out of here! We can't wait for the police!" I pawed through my purse for my keys. Someone tried to pull Big Earl away from the vault door, but he flung them away.

"You are FIRED!" he screamed at the door, spittle coating his chin. "You will never work in this town again. Do you hear me?" He obviously wasn't going to be any help.

"Come on Ashley! Snap out of it!" I yelled and ran over to where she was moaning and rocking on the floor.

"No, no. Leave me here," she moaned and tried to shake me off.

"Not a chance, cream puff," I tugged her up to wrap her little chicken arm around my shoulder. "Let's go!" I dragged her to the door. "Theresa, is that your Suburban outside?" She nodded grimly and grabbed her keys as the chainsaw started to come through the heavy wooden door.

We ran out the front, but I could see we wouldn't all fit into Theresa's SUV, no matter how much we squished. Plus, I couldn't lift Ash to get her in on top of everyone else. I made a split-second decision and drug her over to my graduation present instead, an little Nissan Sentra, so old it had manual locks and windows. I fumbled with my door key, getting it open only to realize the windows were down.

"Well shit." I managed to stuff an unresponsive Ashley into the passenger seat. She tried to get out, so I locked her in while the others all packed into the Suburban. I heard a scream and looked back at the bank in time to see blood spatter on the corner window and then Psycho barged through the front door, yelling and shaking the chainsaw over his head like a caveman.

I pulled up the lock on my door and got in, fumbling the keys again when I tried to start the car. My hands were shaking so bad that I dropped them on the floor mat.

I picked up the keys and jammed them into the ignition, looking up to see him running toward my open window, yanking at the starter cord. Ashley squeaked and shrank into her door, grasping for the door handle and moaning. I jammed my feet on the pedals and turned the key as the saw came roaring back to life, straight out of my nightmares.

Don't stall! Don't stall! I jammed my foot on the accelerator and leaned away from the maniac at my window. I made myself let out the clutch slowly even as the chainsaw descended toward me and I yanked the wheel to the right as we lurched away from him. We scraped the car next to us with a screech and a shudder but managed to pull away just in time.

We were speeding toward the exit, Ashley moaning and curled into a fetal ball against the door, when I looked in my rearview mirror and saw that the SUV hadn't moved. Psycho Killer advanced on his new target and raised the saw high over his head once more. He brought it down on Theresa's driver side door with a terrible screeching noise and sparks as metal met metal. I saw terrified faces inside and slammed on my breaks without thinking.

"What are you doing?" Ashley snapped out of it long enough to scream at me.

"Helping Bev," I growled, knowing that didn't make much sense. Bev was dead. I threw my little car in reverse, scowling into my rearview mirror at Psycho next to the Suburban. I threw my arm over the passenger seat and my foot hovered over the accelerator. Ash screamed and clung to the door as I slammed my foot on the gas. I accelerated straight toward them just as Psycho Killer raised his chainsaw above his head and howled to the sky.

I plowed right into him, crashing into the back corner of the SUV with him in the middle. The chainsaw flew from his hands, hitting the roof of the SUV as it sputtered and died before hitting the asphalt on the other side.

I finally took my foot off the gas and turned off the engine. I left him pinned between the vehicles, slumping over the trunk of my car. I felt weirdly focused and calm as I set the parking break, got out and retrieved the tire iron that had been sliding around behind my seat ever since I got the car.

Psycho Killer had his eyes open and was squirming when I got to him, blood dripping from his mouth.

"This is for Bev," I said and swung the tire iron like a baseball bat at his head as hard as I could. There was a dull whump and blood spattered the SUV's back passenger window.

I wiped my forehead with the back of my hand and realized I still had the tire iron gripped in my fist. I couldn't seem to make myself drop it. I met Ash's wide-eyed stare in the side mirror of my poor little destroyed car.

"You ok?" I asked. "Everyone ok?" I yelled to the occupants of the SUV as Terrell's Trans Am squealed into the parking lot. He jumped out with his gun drawn, but quickly stuck in his waistband at the small of his back as he took in the scene.

"Jeez, Janie," he came over to me as reality kicked in and I started shaking. He pried the tire iron from my hand and wrapped his arms around me.

A car door slammed. "Well, well, well. Isn't that just sweet?" Ashley's angry voice sounded from behind me. Terrell let go of me like he was burned.

"Ash? Baby, what are you doing here? Are you ok?" he asked. "Whoa, Baby whoa! What are you doing?" I turned to see her pointing a small handgun at us.

"Don't move. None of you in there move!" she yelled at Theresa and the rest of the bank crew in the SUV. "Put your arms back around her Terrell. That's how I want to remember you both when I shoot you," she said, her face livid, but her eyes cold. He slowly put his arms around me again.

"You thought I didn't know?" she asked. "You two thought you could screw around behind my back all this time and I wouldn't figure it out? Do you see all this?" she screeched and gestured around us. "My father? All the people dead at the Dairy Royale? It's all your fault."

"Ash, sweetheart? What are you saying?" Terrell asked in shock.

"Don't sweetheart me, you asshole! This is all your fault! If you could've just kept your pants zipped none of this would have happened. I wouldn't have had to hire him to kill her." She pointed first at Psycho Killer, now slumped with a definitely lopsided skull over the trunk of my little car, then at me, still very much alive at least for the moment.

"But no, even after that first time, you two still couldn't keep your clothes on! I had to pawn all my jewelry, my new Rolex! All to get him to come back and finish the job on your little piece of ass, Terrell!" she shook with anger. She seemed more upset about the jewelry than about the death of her own father.

And apparently, I was the only one of Terrell's girls that she'd found out about. I wondered what she'd do if I told her the truth. I was so focused on Ashley and the gun pointed at me, I barely noticed the sound of gears grinding somewhere nearby. I needed a plan. I needed to get to Terrell's gun.

"You paid him again when he didn't finish the job the first time? Isn't that a big no-no when hiring a contractor?" I asked to cover my movement as I angled my body a little into Terrell's.

"Shut up!" she screeched at me. "You don't talk! It's my turn now." Ok, maybe taunting the crazy girl wasn't my best plan.

"I am so done with you Terrell! We're through! This is the last straw, you riding in to her rescue like a black knight in that piece of shit car! You didn't even know I was here!" She squared her shoulders and brought her other hand up to steady the gun. "I'm going to do what I should have done in the first place. I'm going to shoot you both myself."

Any moment now, she was going to pull that trigger. I pretended to cringe into Terrell's chest, feigning weakness to turn him a little more so she couldn't see his back. I dropped my head to his shoulder and pretended to cry as I inched my right hand around his waistband.

"Aw, is poor little Janie-bitch scared now?" she mocked in a sing-song voice. Terrell tensed as I curled my hand around the handle of his gun. "Good, you should be you slut!" she screamed, looking completely unhinged. I could now hear police sirens, finally getting closer in the distance, and a rumbling noise I didn't try to place.

I watched in horror as her finger tightened on the trigger. Terrell yanked us both to the ground at the same time that I drew his gun, pointed it at Ashley, and pulled the trigger. Her gun went off and a plate glass window across Main Street shattered behind us. Ashley recoiled with a cute shriek, but all the gun in my hand did was click. Click, click. I tried again. Nothing.

She recovered, smirked, and aimed again. We rolled and a bullet dug into the asphalt where my head had been. A chip of pavement bit into my cheek.

Terrell swore and grabbed for the gun. "Shit, Janie! The safety!" He flicked it off and aimed at his girlfriend, only to recoil as Psycho Killer's big rig plowed right past us and into Ashley.

"Spawn of the devil!" Ms. Bitchell screamed as she leaned out the driver's window.

Ashley was knocked clear out into the street and directly into the path of a wailing police car.

The officer had no time to even swerve and his car ran her over with a th-thump, th-thump before skidding to a stop.

Many hours later, Terrell and I were finally allowed to leave the police station with a gruff warning not to leave town. The bank employees had all been questioned and allowed to leave hours ago. All except our rescuer, Ms. Bitchell, who was being held on charges of killing the town princess.

"You need a ride home?" Terrell asked. I rubbed the back of my neck wearily and thought of my destroyed little car. I'd only had it two weeks.

I nodded. "Yeah." He slung an arm around my shoulders and walked me to his car. His parents had brought his Trans-Am over from the bank and were waiting behind it in their mini-van to follow Terrell home. I'd called Dad but he hadn't answered, probably passed out in his recliner with a bottle nearby.

"So," he slid his hand down my leg on the way home and gave my knee a squeeze. "We still on for tonight?" He gave me his customary smirk. What a douche. After all we'd been through today…. I blew out a breath. Who was I kidding?

"Sure," I gave him a smirk of my own. I really had to get out of this town.

The Small

The Red Hat Man

Maybe its a new...

this thinking that I do...

keeps haunting me back...

It's a world full of bodies,

each one with a brain,

the brain a person,

every person,

person.

What is the count?

What is the purpose?

Just to live?

Become bigger than?

Survive?

Evolve?

Take advantage of?

One person

on a rock

with nothing around

seems kinda pointless.

Except we are more than one,

we dream.

Each dream owned individually,

driving somewhere.

Lives are not mapped

no plans made before existence.

So...

Why do it at all?

No idea where the journey leads,

each choice a cross road

until the choices are gone

results being a death bed.

Reason and Reasons,

Love, Joy, Control, Power, Peace, Harmony, Learning, Wisdom, Comfort, Competition,

Again each one so small

but together they are one life.

of billions

The small.

Speedos and Sixth Graders

Josh Kilen

When I was 12 years old, my Dad managed to embarrass me more than I ever dreamed possible by deploying a smallish Speedo, some heretofore untapped middle-aged bravado, and then traipsing before my entire 6th grade class. It was certainly a night to remember.

One of the highlights of my private Lutheran middle school years was an annual tournament creatively named Lutheran Elementary School Tournament, or LEST for short. LEST was a pre-pubescent bacchanalia of young protestants battling in diverse events such as knowledge bowls, spelling bees, volleyball, and basketball tournaments. It was a Northwest Lutheran's equivalent of the World Cup.

In addition to the competitions, LEST was a prime opportunity for heady teenage hormones to go a little wild. With more than 15 schools staying in the same hotels, it was an excellent opportunity to find young people of the opposite sex and then stare at them awkwardly. Often the best place to find a large cluster of young people was the pool, which was why two nights into the event my friend Robbie and I were chomping at the bit to go down for a look. Visiting a pool filled with girls from other schools was about as close to James Bond strolling into a Montenegro Casino and seducing foreign beauties as we were likely to get at that age. The imagined possibilities were truly endless.

Primed with our swimsuits and towels, feeling pretty confident in ourselves, we were at the door when my Mom delivered some terrible news.

"Oh, boys! Wait up, your father and sisters are coming with you," she said.

To a 12 year old hoping to catch the notice of and perhaps, maybe, even talk to a pretty girl from another school, this was the kiss of death. Invariably I would be put in charge of my sisters' safety and my great plans of lust and love would never bear fruit. We slumped on the bed and in unison let out deep lip sputtering sighs to wait for them.

My sisters changed in the other room and my father went to the bathroom. The girls were surprisingly swift, re-entering our room with shrill and excited laughter, but my Dad was taking his time. One thing I learned early in life, there's no hurrying my Dad in the bathroom. So we waited.

The door opened and we hoped off the bed excitedly. My Dad emerged from the bathroom with what I can only describe as a flourish. There he was, barely covered in the smallest bathing suit I have ever had the misfortune of seeing. It was a tiny black thread of a thing, with enough fabric around the groin to be considered, technically, legal. It's main purpose from what we could see, which was all too much, was to leave very little to the imagination.

"Oh Craig! No!" My mother rightly exclaimed.

"What?" my father said, attempting to look sincerely befuddled, without fully managing to conceal his glee.

"You cannot wear that to the pool," my mother said. Her face betrayed obvious concern that the man she had pledged to love forever was capable of such bad decision-making.

"We agree with Mom!" We all said in unison, even my friend who was, of course, now bonded to our family for life.

"It's fine, it covers everything." he said, meeting our uncomfortable stares head on. As though it would somehow make matters clear he added, "This is the only suit I brought." Whether it was the presence of my friend, or my sisters' horrified expressions, I'll never know, but with slight acquiescence to our silent pleading he said, "Fine, I'll put on a robe until we get down there and slip into the pool so no one will see." With surprising swiftness he grabbed a robe, threw it on, and motioned us toward the door. "Come on! The pool awaits," he said cheerfully. Words that had just a moment before held so much promise suddenly filled me with a terminal dread.

We walked down the hallway as though filing toward an executioner and rode the elevator down in silence. No one wanted to acknowledge the situation. I prayed that this was the one time of day that no one from my school, or God willing any school, would be at the pool. The doors opened and we walked out of the elevator directly into the pool area.

My prayers were not answered. It seemed that Robbie and I had missed a memo somewhere because my entire class was in the pool, splashing around and generally carrying on like 12 year olds do. Only a few noticed us, waving their hellos as they dived back into the mass of arms and legs. We tentatively walked to the edge of the pool, quickly found places for our towels and dove in. My sisters did the same.

Dad, however, had a different agenda. With an uncharacteristic enthusiasm and showmanship, he whipped off his robe and threw it off towards our towels with a sort of wild abandon. I don't know if it was his intention, but all activity in the pool ceased. Not a word whispered, not a ripple was made. All eyes were now glued to my Dad and his barely-there-European-style bathing suit. Let me tell you, looking up at my Dad in a Speedo was not a superior view.

A young man swam up behind me, Rick, the class doorknob, (you know, the one everyone hates, but follows anyway), and said, "Hey, isn't that your Dad?"

"I,…. uh,….. uh,……" I stammered, face burning with humiliation. Most twelve year old boys are not equipped to handle complex social situations like these, and I was no exception.

"Dork," Rick said as he splashed the side of my face. With the ice sufficiently broken, the pool came back to life as everyone shifted their attention from my father's package to their previous activities. Albeit their distraction was evident in the constant glances back to my Dad's nearly nude physique.

In response to the extra attention, my father decided to do possibly the worst thing a middle aged man wearing a tiny bathing suit around almost teenagers could do; he stretched. Arms spread, he arched his back, and thrust his hips forward like a cocked bow . I looked up, mouth agape at his audacity. Then I noticed the looks on the faces of the moms lounging around the pool. It was a mixture of admiration and horror. Oblivious to this, He entered the water and started playing with my sisters as if everything was normal.

Over the next twenty minutes, those quietly appreciative Lutheran mothers led their children away from the pool area. They each left with a parting glance at my Dad and I knew that we were they reason they hastened their exit. Eventually we were the only ones left in the pool.

I was thoroughly embarrassed and I don't ever recall being more angry with my Dad. To my adolescent sense of justice, it seemed like the most selfish thing I had ever witnessed. Twenty-two years later, I think I understand his decisions a little better.

At the time my father was 36 years old and had been working out steadily for over a year. He was struggling to overcome the dreaded middle age flabby look that many of his friends had succumbed to and he succeeded admirably. So, at 36, with the toned body of a teenager, my Dad just wanted to show off a little. Why he chose to display his new physique to a group of nearly teenagers and their parents will always be a mystery, but as a 34 year old man looking down at a decidedly larger belly, I think I understand my Dad's motivations a little better.

Eulogy

Perry Buto

I met him on the train to Tule Lake. Mama was annoyed with the American government for taking us from our San Francisco farm at the beginning of our summer harvest, but she made us go and get the guard so we could feed him lunch. "This war is not his fault," she whispered in Japanese. "And that poor boy probably hasn't eaten all day! Kazuo! I brought an extra obentou. Go get the soldier, and I'll feed him!" My older brother called the soldier in, and took his place.

Kazu winked at me from outside the door, his brown eyes gleaming mischievously, and "Make sure that soldier gets fed full up! I'll hold his gun and play Cowboys and Indians out here!" I nodded and ran over to help Mama. Our compartment's soldier was a young, blond man with laughing, blue eyes.

"'Scuse me, would you happen to have a kerchief I could use?" The soldier asked, breaking the companionable silence that had fallen over our train car.

"Certainly," I said, handing him the green, hand-stitched handkerchief I kept in my tunic pocket. He was not a neat eater, and I figured I could suffice without it. "Please, keep it."

"Oh!" He looked very surprised, "but didn't you make this?"

"I did," I responded. "But I have others, so please feel free."

He smiled at me, "Thanks kindly!"

"Your accent is interesting; I've never heard it before," I said after a moment.

"Well, then, you've never been to the South. I'm from Georgia."

"Oh," I said.

My youngest sister, Chizue—who was four, and had the rosiest, red-apple cheeks and cutest bowl-shaped haircut—teetered up to the blond man and touched his knee as he struggled to use his chopsticks, "How come can't use? Ohashi easy."

"Chie!" I said, "That's rude! Leave him alone to eat in peace." Chie looked back and forth between the soldier and me; she was genuinely curious, but mother had taught us that we should never be rude.

"Don't worry, miss," the young man said to me with a lopsided grin, "she's cute, and I can tell she don't mean any harm."

"Sorry for her broken English. She's fluent in Japanese, and has only started to pick up on English recently."

He smiled at me, "My name is Alastair. Alastair Freeman. You can call me 'Al.' It's nice to meet you…"

"Hanako Abe," I filled in bashfully. "This is my mother, and this is my sister, Chizue. My older brother, Kazuo, is the one who called you in."

"Well then, hello, Abe family, and thanks for the meal! I've never had such delicious Japanese food!"

I turned to Mama. "He said that the food is excellent," I said in Japanese.

"Ah!" She turned toward Al and bowed, "Arigatou gozaimashita." Thank you very much.

"Oh," I realized that he might not understand. "She said—"

He stood up and bowed in return, "Douitashimashite." You are welcome.

We all fell silent as he placed his empty bento box and chopsticks in a little pile on the floor. With a tip of his hat and a twinkle in his eye, he said, "There was a Japanese grandmother who lived next door, so I know a few words here and there, but, sadly, she always fed me with a fork." With that, Al gave Kazu a firm pat on the back and ushered him into the train car, taking back the rifle, and returning to his post.

Our train car was silent until a few hours later when the camp's bell tower became visible, its exposed bell hanging heavy against the steel rafters, and Mama finally spoke, "He seems like a nice boy, Hanako. He would make a good husband—even if he isn't Japanese."

"Mama!"

***

We had arrived at Tule Lake early in the summer of 1942—and, since Kazu had refused to fill out his loyalty questionnaire, as he had been afraid he'd end up drafted into the army leaving the rest of us to fend for ourselves, we all stayed in the camp with everyone else deemed "disloyal" by the government—and by the winter of 1943 we were quite settled. Although we were used to chilly California winters, our quarters lacked central heating, so we had to find our own ways to keep warm. The barracks we lived in were small enough that the four of us took up the entire shack, and, by some happy coincidence, Al was one of the main patrolmen for our area. He came over frequently—I found out later that he was friendly to all of the other families, but it was only ours he would visit regularly.

"It's nice to take a break," he would say, looking up wistfully to the pale blue sky. But I saw the growing number of bruises on his arms, the fluctuating sizes of his uniform, and the increasingly poor state of his boots. I never asked, because it wasn't my business, but I also noticed the looks the other soldiers would give him when he left our barracks. Though Mama was worried that he would get caught and discharged for conspiring, he insisted on bringing us small candies or trinkets every time, even after martial law had been imposed. Every time he gave us something, he asked for something in return: a single story of our life before camp.

Chie always talked about food, Kazu always talked about the farm and yard work, and I always talked about family. One day, he brought me a canned juice—it was cranberry, and it was a real treat—and asked me about my father.

"What happened to him?" Al asked.

I felt my throat burn as I swallowed back the ache in my chest. "His elbows and knees swelled, he itched something terrible, and collapsed in the fields. Kazu found him lying there after Mama called us in for dinner. I… we… buried him beneath his favorite peach tree, and Kazu made me and Chie promise not to talk about it with Mama." I put the can of juice down next to me. I wasn't thirsty anymore.

"Oh," he said quietly. "I'm sorry."

"Yeah," I said as I stared at the green kerchief neatly sticking out of his pocket. "So am I." He never asked about it again, and I was grateful.

A few weeks later, Chie fell ill. She had been slowly eating less and less, and complained of stomach troubles, but Mama had simply pursed her lips tightly together and silently watched, and Al—perceptive man that he was—brought Chie some stomach tonics, which she started taking every morning.

"I really don't think Chie should go to school today, Mama," I said after a week of silent endurance. I heard Chie's muffled whimpers, and watched as she rubbed her inflamed elbows.

"If Chizue says she will go, we will let her." Mama said without looking up from her quilting. I glared at the tightly-pulled, grey bun that sat on the top of her head, unable to bring myself to glower at her directly.

"But Mama! It's so cold outside! She won't last!"

"Ask her if she wants to go, and if she does, we will let her. It is for her own good to go to school, Hanako." Her lips were smashed into a thin line, but I saw the gentle tremor in her fingertips as she sewed. Everything was so familiar, and I knew that I had promised Kazu years ago that I wouldn't say anything, but I couldn't help it.

"Mama, I know that you can see that this is just like when Papa—"

"Hanako," she said quickly, throwing a sharp glance up at me. "Many good people have already died, and you must be prepared to lose everything too. Let her at least be happy." Mama was so pale, and I saw the helplessness in the slight slump of her shoulders. I was still angry, but I was ashamed for forgetting that Mama was suffering just like the rest of us.

"Fine," I said, relenting. "Just—fine."

"You have too much American fire, Hanako. Now, go ask her."

"Yes please," Chizue responded groggily when I asked her. I grabbed her arms—they were dark and swollen like ripe grapes and freckled with a pond-ripple rash, "School please." My throat fogged with the threat of tears—I saw Papa's empty eyes staring right back at me through her—but I let her go to school.

Just before lunch, there were screams coming from the elementary school yard, and I was called out of my classroom.

Chie had collapsed.

The teachers said that she had wobbled a bit, coughed, and then fell over and seized violently.

Kazu had also been called from class, and Mama had been called from our quarters. I looked at Chie's swollen face, and felt Papa's wheezing kiss on my forehead, saw his bloated skin puckered tightly against his white tunic as he went out to work in the farm for the last time. I wondered if this is how Kazu found Papa—dead, but still twitching—in the fields under the hot sun. While attending medical school over a decade later, I figured out that they had both died of Rheumatic Fever most likely brought on by poor genetics and weak hearts. Kazu's left hand held his sobs in, while his right tenderly ghosted through Chie's sweaty angel-hair.

Underneath the watchful eyes of the unmoving bell tower that slowly swallowed our hopes, we had a small funeral. Our family, a couple of Chie's friends and their parents, and Al attended. Most of us didn't bother going to funerals anymore unless we were directly related to the deceased. Mama silently placed a dried rice cracker at the base of Chie's grave, and pressed her lips together tightly. Kazuo and I quietly threw pretty weeds that we had plucked from the schoolyards, and huddled together to stave off the cold. Al tossed Chie's favorite candy into her grave, and sobbed louder than I'd ever heard a man cry before.

***

The following spring at Tule Lake, after martial law had ended and the number of barracks in the camp had been increased, I was one of the many set to graduate high school—a chance I never would have had while we were on the farm. I was 21, but I was not the oldest in the class, and I was the best at arithmetic. On the morning of my graduation, I was talking to Mama about the outfit I wanted to wear.

"I would like to have a new skirt apron, since I can't buy a new dress for the occasion. May I borrow your sewing kit and have some of the cloth Al brought you last week?" Mama smiled and chuckled quietly.

"No. That cloth is a precious gift, and I was planning to make a new curtain for Kazuo's bed."

"What!? But I'm only going to have one graduation! C'mon, Kazu, you understand!" I turned to Kazu, but he was not listening. He had grown gloomy since Chie's death, the crow's-feet at the corners of his eyes morphing into frown lines on his forehead. He hardly spoke anymore, and seemed to drift along throughout the day, like a ghost.

"Kazu!"

"I'm sorry, Hana. Just listen to Mama." He fiddled with a little wooden top with a sloppy "Chizue" scratched into the side. He twirled it, and watched it spin and falter, spin and falter with a sigh. Kazu's weary fingernails scraped across his shaved scalp, scratching half-heartedly at a blemish on the back of his neck.

I did my best impression of Mama, and scrunched my lips together, but he didn't notice. "Fine."

"Hanako, I will make you a new skirt apron once you become a doctor." Mama said.

"But what if I don't get to be a doctor!"

"You will," she promised, with a soft and knowing nod of her head. "I am certain."

In the end, when we headed to the ceremony, there was thick, black smoke oozing from the direction of the school. I ran the whole way there. I found a suffocating orange glow and waves of intense heat that watered my eyes. I watched the fire travel from the school and twinkle up into the sky, unsuccessfully reaching for the bell tower's sturdy, metal frame. Someone had decided to burn down the records center—I wasn't going to get my diploma.

Mama clicked her tongue, turned on her heel, and started back to our quarters. Kazu followed slowly, his hunched back trailing after Mama. I saw them leave, and I couldn't stop my fingers from trembling and my lips pursing together tighter than Mama's ever did. I didn't understand how they could walk away! They should have been just as angry as I was. I saw someone limping toward me from the direction of the fire, and I almost ran away so I couldn't be accused of starting it—many residents of Tule Lake had been executed for less—but I saw scraggly blonde hair and a green kerchief being waved in the air.

"Al!" I called out to him anxiously as he hobbled up to me, "Are you alright!? What happened? Did you see anything or anyone? OH MY GOD! Your eye—!"

"Shush, Hana," he said, still grinning and slightly winded. He pointed to his left eye, which was as purple as a healthy eggplant, "This is where the bastard who set the fire punched me. I managed to break his leg, to keep him from getting away, though! It was a real tough tussle." He coughed, taking a moment to catch his breath, and placed his shaking hand on my shoulder. "Don't worry, Hana, I got him. Don't you worry." I hesitated a moment, but I couldn't stop myself from hugging him and sobbing into his singed uniform. He held my head to his shoulder; ran his fingers through my long, anger-tangled hair; and rubbed circles on my back like Mama should have.

"There, there," he hushed. "I'm sorry you didn't get to graduate."

***

Al was relocated to bell tower watch duty after the school fire; he never said why, but I could see the dirty looks the rest of the guards gave him whenever he waved to one of us. I did, however, feel safer knowing Al was in charge of tower duty—a lot of people did, since they knew he was unlikely to shoot the children who wandered past the gates, unlike most of the soldiers—and, even though it meant that he couldn't visit as often, I knew he kept an eye out for us.

Many camps had begun to release internees in 1945, but the imprisonment didn't end for us until the spring of 1946. All of the residents of Tule Lake—soldiers and prisoners alike—had been on edge since the releases began, praying for an end to the horror we all had begun to believe would be permanent.

I was walking home from the fields when I saw a soldier limp over to Al and begin talking to him. Although their gestures at first seemed innocuous, in a few moments, the limping man grabbed Al by his arm. I called out to him, and Al and the soldier turned to look down at me. Alastair smiled apologetically, and the soldier's face contorted in disgust before, in a moment, it changed into a lewd grin.

"Do you wanna know what happens to Jap lovers?" The man screeched down at me. He let go of Al's arm, picked up the shotgun by the guard post, and pointed it at Al's chest. "Hold still, Private Freeman!"

I screamed as he pulled the trigger, but everything was suddenly swallowed by the cacophonous tolling of the bell and the following uproarious cheers from the freed men and women in the fields and the barracks. Startled by the sudden knell, Al stumbled backward toward the railing, was knocked over by the force of the gunshot, and began the long decent toward the dirt.

His fall was graceful and, I swear, he twisted in midair just to look at me. If I hadn't known there was nothing but concrete and soil below my feet, I might have thought that he was an Olympic diver, or an acrobat. I counted each of his teeth twice over as he semi-consciously turned to grin at me, but the acceptance in his eyes reminded me that he was dying.

I watched his body shatter a few feet in front of me. His fingers touched the dirt first, followed by the bones in his forearms snapping and vaulting out of his elbows. I didn't look away when his eyes went dull after the crunch of his head and torso crumbing onto the earth because he gave me so much, and the least I could do was respect him in his last moments—he wouldn't be alone in death like my father had been. I watched his green handkerchief stain deep brown as his life washed away.

"Hana!" Kazu came running from the barracks. "Can you believe it? We're free—OH GOD! Is that—don't look! Let's get you out of here!"

He pulled on my arm, but I couldn't let him take me. "The soldier shot him, Kazu. Because of us." I don't remember starting to cry, but I must have because I was suddenly pulled into the familiar warmth of Kazu's itchy, cotton tunic.

"It's not your fault, Hana. It's not your fault." Kazu whispered as he ushered me away, but I didn't feel guilty. I felt lonely. I would free from here, but Alastair wouldn't—he would be here forever, like Chie. Alastair had been the only good thing in the camp, and now his blood was mixed into the soil and forever stigmatized by the bitter hatred he had worked so hard to counteract.

Stuck

Joshua Swainston

"I can't do this. I'm moving to Portland," Craig announced toward the cubical partition. He arrived at his desk ten minutes prior, confronted with a heaping pile of manila inner-office envelopes. Each package contained a series of job orders which Craig was tasked to individually input, arrange, verify, send to his supervisor, retrieve with revision notes, correct, adjust for continuity, audit, present to committee, then resubmit to his supervisor before moving the job to a "completed" file where it would be scrutinized by the Accounting Department.

"You're not going anywhere," Steven said from the other side of the half-wall.

Craig furrowed his brow. "Fuck you. You don't know. I could. I could go today. Leave for lunch and never come back. Tomorrow you'll come in and HR'll already have some other asshole sitting in my spot."

"Why do you want to go to Portland? It's not exotic or anything. You live in the Northwest already. The only difference between Washington and Oregon is Oregon doesn't have a sales tax. Oh, and they have go-go dancers everywhere. Set your sights a little higher. Hawaii, Costa Rica, Los Angeles, I don't know."

"I want to see what I can do away from … this. Portland seems like a nice mid-step. Plus Portland's cool, right? Art, culture, that kinda shit. There's a show about it on IFC. What do we have? Gray's Anatomy? No thank you." Craig shrugged. "I mean, Katherine Heigl, okay, right? But not the rest of that bullshit.

From Steven's cube came the single word, "Frasier."

"Yeah, Frasier. You're right. I forgot about that one."

Two women at the coffee machine discussed an upcoming baby shower for one of the secretaries on another floor.

Steven rolled his office chair back so he could face his co-worker. The two were stationed on one corner of a cubical honeycomb bordered by managers' glass offices and conference rooms. "Calm down. Step back from the ledge. Everyone does this now and again."

"You mean, freak out?" Craig bugged his eyes and waved his hands putting extra emphasis on 'freak out'.

"It's normal. Be happy for the dream, but don't take too much stock in it. It's the dreaming that makes system work."

"What?"

"This." Steven motioned to the rest of the office. "We're all relatively middle class. We have health care. We wear business-casual attire. Every once in a while management buys lunch for the office. It's not a bad gig. What makes it work is that we all believe there is something better or different we want out there. It's the dreaming that keeps people like us uninterested in moving up to the next level in whatever field. If you are thinking about going to Portland, you aren't thinking about becoming a manager, are you?"

"You know I don't give a shit about that kinda thing. It would be nice for the money, but I'm not management material."

"There's a job opening in Accounts Payable, if you're looking for a change."

"I don't think you're getting the point."

"Really man, what are you complaining about? This company provides a sensible job with good benefits and little to no responsibility. In exchange you do some menial, thoughtless job." Steven considered his word choice. "Maybe 'thoughtless' is the wrong word. How about, 'simple decision making.' In the hierarchy, we're one step above manual labor. That's not so bad. Could be worse, right?"

Craig counted on his left hand fingers as he listed, "So it goes: toilet cleaning, fast food, assembly line, construction, corporate billing. I feel so much better. Thanks. I'm moving to Portland."

"It's noble, isn't it? The idea of the working middle class. The apex of the American Dream. You went to college. You got a job. You're looking at buying a house. By all modern standards, you've won."

"This can't be winning. Whatever this is, it is not winning."

"Don't let Mr. Keen hear you say that." Steven reminded his coworker, then pointed to the ceiling where a black dome hung containing a surveillance system.

"Fuck Mr. Keen."

"Fine." Steven crossed his arms and leaned back in his ergonomic office chair. "If you do go to Portland, what'll you do?"

"You know the one thing that I always regretted not knowing how to do? Unicycle. I'll get a unicycle in Portland."

"You get a unicycle, I'll buy you three bowling pins. You can come up with a juggling street act. That'll be good. Try to get a girlfriend when you list your profession on your Tinder profile as street performer."

Craig turned back to his computer and started clicking around on the desktop. "Thanks for the support. I'm glad that I have you as a friend. If it weren't for you, I might have actually gone off and enjoyed myself. This is what truly sucks about this place, no one can be honest with the people you work with. I say I want to ride a unicycle and you make jokes. Do you know anyone around here, really? Do you really know anything about Sally? You've talked to her every day for three years. Or Jessica, do we know if Jessica likes football or crochet or Japanese movies or whatever? We don't know shit about each other. We're a bunch of closeted strangers unable to talk to one another because we're afraid of being rejected. I don't want to do it anymore."

"Whoa cowboy, cool your spurs. I'm just being realistic." Craig did not respond. Steven continued to hover in the interim between the two semi-private work stations. "Hey man, I didn't mean to piss you off like that. How about I buy lunch today to make it up to you?"

"I'm not hungry."

"It's like Office Space, ya know, case of the Mondays. You'll get over it."

The mention of Office Space reinvigorated Craig. "Do you remember that movie? How did they finally get out of the dead end job?"

"Didn't they embezzle money from the company?" asked Steven.

"No, the building burnt down. Due to some string of coincidences, the building burnt down. And what's worse, out of three main characters, only one of them saw the fire as a way to reinvent themselves. The other two just kept doing the same thing. How fucking sad is that. It's a good movie with a great soundtrack, true, but Office Space, at its core is a sad, sad film."

Laughter erupted from a knot of well-dressed thirty-something's on the other side of the office's floor.

"I give up. You can be all mister Portland and continue on this pity party. I'll be over in my little cubical, going over my day-to-day, enjoying the fact that I'm doing just fine." Steven wheeled back behind the partition.

Craig stood up from his desk, "Dude, Steven, I'm gonna get some air. I'm a bit out of sorts, ya know. I'll be back." It was the closest thing to an apology as he could muster. Steven didn't respond.

Craig took the elevator to the ground floor then out towards 4th Ave. He walked around in the midst of Seattle, got a Pepsi, and sat on a wood park bench under the small-leaf maples in Westlake Park. He wished for a sign, something from an exterior force to tell him what to do. Maybe an unicyclist? That would have made everything clear. Instead he saw the homeless passed out in the crooks of the stone commercial buildings. He saw early morning commuters traversing the city in a hurried attempt to be on time to someplace they would rather not be. Nearby, a panhandler played "Margaritaville" on an acoustic guitar. The world kept on moving. No one was truly happy. Maybe Steven was right? After all he was the byproduct of social evolution, why not go with it. Once resigned, he got up and walked back to the metal and glass tower that housed his job.

"There he is sir," said Steven as Craig exited the elevator. The 'sir' was Mr. Keen, a short, thin man in a dark blue suit.

"And where have you been, Craig?" Asked Mr. Keen.

Craig looked down to make eye contact with his 5'1" boss. "I wasn't feeling so good. I needed some air, so I went for a walk."

"Is that all?" Mr. Keen rubbed his chin.

"Yes, sir," replied Craig.

Mr. Keen pointed at a black dome hanging from a ceiling less than a yard from Craig's desk. "You do know we have cameras in our office?"

"Yes, sir."

"What concerns me is not your absence from your desk. I understand that my employees need a breather now and again. That is why we have quiet rooms available if you so need." Mr. Keen kept eye contact with Craig while pointing to a door on the opposite side of the office. Craig knew that to be the 'quiet room', a place where employee could meditate and reflect away from the rigors of office life. To his knowledge, no employee had ever used the room. "What concerns me is your wellbeing. Steven here tells me you are thinking about relocating to Portland. Is that true?"

Craig was not sure how to answer the question. "It was just a thought, but it sounds alright, I guess."

"You guess, huh? I reviewed the video. You said you wanted to go to Portland and buy a unicycle."

"Why did you ask if you already knew?" The longer Craig spoke to Mr. Keen, the more he felt lost.

"I wanted to know what you'd say."

"And?"

Mr. Keen took a deep breath, "Your wellbeing Craig. Your wellbeing." The short man pulled Craig's desk chair from the desk and took a seat. "See, I'm just a cog like you, a slightly bigger cog, but a cog. It's my job to make sure that the smaller cogs under my supervision keep moving in the right direction. The bigger cogs rely on me to do my job. It's how the whole thing works. Now if one of these little cogs gets loose or is missing a spoke, well at this company we don't just toss the cog aside. We may replace it, true, but we don't discard our valued parts without an attempt at remedying. Do you understand what I'm talking about?"

Steven stood at attention, watching.

Craig shrugged. "Kinda?"

"Good," continued Mr. Keen. "So we are on the same page. Now let's talk about what we are going to do to help our little loose cog. What I think is that maybe our cog might need a little refurbishment. Craig, all of our cogs are valuable, that is why we offer such a great place to work."

"Okay, sir, I think you lost me."

"See, that is what I'm afraid of, losing you. Now I don't want that to happen. You said something that truly concerned me. When I saw you leave on the video, I came down to talk to Steven just to make sure I heard you correctly. Do you know what that thing was?"

Craig scanned the office and counted the black hanging domes. Twelve in total, watching everyone on the floor. "Was it when I said 'Fuck Mr. Keen'?"

"No, I cannot concern myself with my own popularity. I'm here looking after the good of the company as a whole." Mr. Keen gave a deep sigh. "I don't think you are following. Let's go back to the cogs, shall we? You seem to be doing better with the cogs."

"Okay."

"Do you know what happens to the other cogs when one cog gets a chip in a spoke?" Mr. Keen kept a blank face while teaching his subordinate.

"I don't know much about mechanics, sir," answered Craig.

"Do you know, Steven?" asked Mr. Keen.

"Yes, sir." Steven smiled as he answered. "When one cog is chipped then it causes other cogs to wear unevenly and chip as well."

"That's right Steven," Mr. Keen acknowledged. "It's infectious. One chip leads to unforeseen wear and damage throughout the entire machine. That is why we feel it is needed that we take these issue causing cogs and get them fixed. So when I heard you say 'this is not winning' it concerned me. By our research, you should be happy enough in your profession. So why aren't you?"

"Maybe I'm tired," Craig suggested.

The other employees on the floor seemed to have taken no notice of the entire exchange.

Mr. Keen nodded. "If that's the problem then that is something we can work on."

"So what are 'we' going to work on?" asked Craig.

"When was the last time you read your employment agreement?" Mr. Keen reached out to Steven who placed a several page document into his hand. "In article thirteen, under health and moral, mental or physical, it states that at any time if said employee demonstrates a subpar mindset as to corrupt the efficacy of the workplace, then said employee should be sanctioned to treatment under the recommendation of the employee's supervisor."

Mr. Keen's words felt like ugly mush against Craig's mind. "Can I quit?"

"Not without an exit interview, I'm afraid. For that, you need to be in your right mind. The fact that you want to quit demonstrates to me that at this juncture you are not." A company security guard positioned himself behind Craig. "No, as part of our very wonderful medical coverage, you'll be admitted to Western State Mental Institute for your rest until what time when you can function as a more perfect cog. Of course this is to no expense to you or your family."

"You can't do this."

The security guard placed a hand on Craig's shoulder.

"No, don't worry, we insist." Mr. Keen stood up, passed the employment agreement back to Steven, and returned to his own office to continue monitoring his employees via the closed circuit system. Steven returned to his work.

"You can't do this." Craig repeated, this time to anyone in the office who would listen. Nobody took notice.

The security guard escorted Craig by the arm into the elevator. "You must be crazy," said the guard. "This is the best job I've ever had. You know how much I get paid? It's ridiculous, and the benefits. You don't even get healthcare like this in the military. Why would you ever want to leave?"

Conflict

Justin Racine

In this grey world,

Conflict seems the norm,

From man to nature,

To the bird and the worm.

It doesn't matter

If it is physically waged.

It comes from within and without,

From short to long ranged.

Be they matters of the heart,

Or matters of money and gold.

There is nothing one cannot fight,

To get a close hold.

Not to say that it isn't necessary,

I believe it just should be moderated,

With kindness and compassion,

To not seem like such a mad craven

Sure the violence and discord,

Is to be somewhat frowned upon,

But without it we couldn't have revolutions,

Or learn to let go and move on.

So I ask you people,

To carefully reflect,

On the most natural of concepts,

That one cannot simply reject.

Though it is a cruel truth,

It can lead to happiness,

Trust me for a bit,

It's worth all the sadness.

Rose Garden Cat

Ellen Miffitt

The cat slunk between the shrubs. Low to the ground and keeping his body small, his movements were calculated and precise. His ears pricked forward as the sound reached his new position. Pausing he listened intently. Not recognizing its source, he continued to move cautiously. By the rock stairs, he stopped beneath the wooden bench and tucked into the shadows and waited. Old enough to know not to run directly into the unknown especially at night, he sniffed the air. Licking a front paw, he brushed his face clean. Working over his ears to his whiskers, he froze as the sound washed over him again.

He knew his territory well which included the places to avoid at what time during the day. He especially knew to avoid the children before and after school. He had learned quickly through pain of thrown objects directed at him by the boys. It was always a temptation to visit the garbage dumpster for a quick bite after the children's lunch. Sometimes the cook's assistant left him a special treat. He was wary of most people and kept to himself most of the time. At least there was a leash law and he felt safe from the dogs in the area. As a matter of safety, he knew where climbable trees were just in case.

Time to decide whether to find the cause of the noise; he knew he was close to it but it didn't seem to be coming as regularly as before. The night was moonless and provided him with plenty of cover so he wasn't concerned with his own peril as long as he kept to the darkest places. Thankful for his black coat, he eased from under the bench through a hole in the shrub fence that sheltered this public park garden. This was the part of the garden with sharp thorns on the plants. The summer night was thick with the scent from the low hanging flowers. One section of earth was freshly disturbed. The dampness of the soil filled his nose as he skirted the rectangle of soft dirt; there was also another familiar odor. He retreated to the overhanging Hosta leaves at the end of the bed that wrapped around the trellis bench. Before he even settled on his haunches, the muffled sound arose from almost in front of his feet. Temporally backing further under the large oval leaves he watched the soil move. His nose discerned many fresh smells but among them stood out the smell of the assistant cook. He had smelt her scent on the food dish she smuggled to him at the school. Why did he smell it here among the rose beds?

The rose bushes in this recently turned plot were wilted and limp. The soft earth was easy to move aside. Although dogs were much better diggers, he knew he had to dig deeper than his normal toilet needs dictated. Working the freshly turned soil, he scattered the dirt from where the last movement had cracked the soil. Rapidly his white paws threw soft clumps into the air two feet behind him. His back feet sank into the garden with the effort of his front paws. Closing in on the sound, he was getting nearer to something hard; the woman's scent was encompassed in the soil.

His paws exposed part of her face; she tried to move her head but the dirt collapsed into the small hole he had created. He shifted his position and began again. Between digging furiously he would sit and peer down. Slowly he exposed part of her face enough so that she could turn from side to side. The duct tape was not sticking to her skin. The rose garden's moisture helped insure its release. The cat sat beside her the rest of the night.

The city park gardener's frantic call to 911 on his cell phone momentarily confused the dispatch operator. The poor man kept yelling about finding a cat sitting next to a buried body in the rose garden. The cat backed under the Hosta plants to watch as the gardener wildly yanked the wilted rose bushes aside, pulled away dirt and mulch to reveal more of the woman's bound body. Sirens wailed as police and medics arrived within minutes of his call; police yellow crime scene tape draped the scene. The crime investigation team began photographing, collecting evidence and making notes to solve the crime. Who had attempted to bury the cook's assistant alive in the city park rose bed?

A Haunting

Tiffany Aldrich MacBain

Beyond the golden years of trick-or-treating, Halloween morphs into a high-pressure holiday, like New Year's Eve or the 4th of July, when you feel like you must have plans or else endure a long night of loneliness and self-loathing, a night pierced by the cackling laughter of fun-havers outside your window, a night most unhallowed. If you happen to have plans, your suffering is of another sort: weeks in advance of the party, you have to figure out what you're going to "be." And then you must buy and assemble components of a costume, and then you have to wear it all.

Having a child relieved me of that burden: the moment I dressed my infant as a peapod the focus shifted to her, and because of my ever-advancing age, thank god, I will never attract such attention again unless some darkly or too brightly humored person one day dresses me as a peapod, and by then I will be too far gone to know or care.

I suspect that people who like Halloween are drawn to the lure of the carnivalesque. They want to be someone else for a night, to flout the rules of society and self without reprisal. There's chaos to that behavior; there's chance and misrule. No wonder I don't like it. I've had enough trouble without borrowing more.

Even so, I have tried. I have been game. In college, I convinced my roommate to don a blue blazer and black fedora and to pencil in a thin mustache so that she could be pimp to my prostitute. (Our friend, whose feminism surpassed our own at that time, dressed in black and held a sign condemning our costumes. She stayed by our sides all night.) A year after, having taken a Women's

Studies class and watched a few hours of CSPAN, I borrowed from my mother a satiny Coke can costume and affixed to the top of it a black squiggle of yarn: it was a pubic hair, condemning Clarence Thomas and supporting Anita Hill. And then there were the years of the blond wig. I wore it with prison duds and carried a muffin pan: Martha Stewart. I paired it with press-on nails and tight jeans: Carmela Soprano. For its swan song, the blond wig transformed me into Britney Spears. She and I, pregnant at the same time, were a page out of *US Weekly*, "Who Wore It Best?": sunglasses, pink sweats, shirts that bared midriffs 6-months-swelled, and, in our hands, packs of Kools, venti coffees, and babies not wholly attended to—mine a doll, hers, her son Sean.

Three months after that last Halloween, Britney shaved her head, apparently in the midst of a crackup or maybe to hide traces of drugs in her hair so she wouldn't lose her boys. I was in a hospital room with my infant daughter. She had been born with something wrong, a defect, you could say, although I do not use that word. We had learned about her problem, her father and I, on Halloween, two days after the costume party. "There is no stomach," the ultrasound technician had said. "Maybe she hasn't eaten recently. You can't see the stomach unless there's something in it. Or maybe it's still small." In time we were to learn that our daughter's esophagus was divided in two. She would be born in Seattle so that we'd have easy access to a Neonatal Intensive Care Unit, or NICU, and then she'd be moved to Children's Hospital, where we would live, she and I, until the ends of her esophagus grew close enough together for the surgeons to finish the work that nature had abandoned. This stay would extend for months and then, after a surgical complication that nearly ended her life, months more, a great lonely and frightening swath of time that would cauterize the split between my past self and who I am now.

Who needs Halloween? Every day—I do not exaggerate—I live with fear; I give some thought to my child's life, to her being alive. In the mornings, Thank God she has woken up; when I drop her off at school, Please let her survive this day, let no madman enter this place and kill her; when I put her to bed at night, Is her window locked? Is my door open so that I can hear her call out? I know why this is. It's because once, I left her in a hospital room while I went to have a shower, and while I was gone she almost died. A nurse was there; my mother was there; but even so, an intravenous line had burst my child's superior vena cava and filled her chest cavity and scarred her lungs with poison. Her lower organs had shut down because her blood could not reach them. Her head had swelled because where could the blood go? She lay there, only three months old, dying.

In a way, I saved her. When I saw how she looked—her head too large, a line running across her chest, above it dark red, below it yellow—I ran from the room, searching for the head of the

NICU. I found him amidst a bunch of physicians, leading morning rounds, and I interrupted to say, "Dr. Brogan, something is wrong." Why should he have listened to me? I am an English professor, not a doctor. He is a doctor, and was busy. And already a nurse and a surgical resident had downplayed my concern. But during my week in Intensive Care, he and I had gotten to know each other, had bonded over literature, in fact. (Before med school Dr. Brogan had been an English major: never let it be said that ours is a useless degree.) So he had reason to trust me, and he dropped what he was doing and followed me. They all did. He told me later that the expression on my face had been enough to convince him to come. I looked like I had seen a ghost.

Emily Dickinson wrote, "One need not be a Chamber – to be Haunted – One need not be a House." "The Brain has Corridors" more suitable to ghosts; "Ourself behind ourself, concealed – Should startle most." I am haunted by the events of that morning. I wish they would let me be. In that moment, I was awake, definitive, intent. I acted. Doctors and nurses and technicians acted. My child lived. But it left me with the knowledge that such things can happen: a mother can go to have a shower and, because she hasn't done so all week, take a few extra minutes to apply her makeup, and when she returns, her child might be changed, her child might even be gone. That mother—myself behind myself, concealed—lives in my brain. She doesn't startle me much anymore; I'm used to her rattling around, and I'm learning to limit her circuit. But there she is, and there she'll stay, watching my daughter and waiting, waiting, waking me from my sleep, ever watchful and waiting still.

Bones

Ross Dohrmann

I'll never forget those final days of summer before He left and everything changed. He was always there, always, right after school He'd come home. During the summer, which He said is when the "dog days" are, it was even better because He didn't go to school, so He could play and ruffle my neck like He always did. The last few days He was with me a lot, and laughing, and playing, and so much walking. Then one day He was sad and the next day He was gone.

They think we can't keep track of time, but we can, we do. He left one year, and five months, and thirteen days ago. I knew He was going to go though. He's left before, but I didn't know it would be for one year, and five months, and thirteen days. I know when He's going for a short time and when He's going for a long time. When He goes for a short time He ruffles my neck and smiles, and points, and says to me, "Now, Bucko, you watch the house and take care of Mom." Then I put my paw in his paw and He sits up straight, and then I sit up straight because

He laughs and looks at me when I sit up straight, but I usually look at something else instead of Him. He didn't do that one year, and five months, and thirteen days ago.

The third day before He left, I thought He was going to go for a short time because He started to put his things in bags, and He does that when He goes for a short time. I liked that day because He took me to the lake, and I like going to the lake because that's where I swim. He put his things in bags for a while, and I sat close by and watched just in case He needed my help. After fifteen minutes there were too many bags, so I closed my eyes but didn't sleep. He called my name and He had his ball glove. He looked at it, then at me, and put it in a bag, which made me happy because He likes playing ball and I like playing ball too.

"You're going to have to help me get through the next couple of days, okay?" He said. I cocked my head.

It took a little longer to get to the lake that day because He went slowly in the car. Usually we get to the lake in seventeen minutes, but the third day before He left we got there in twenty-three minutes. I didn't mind though because it was warm that day and the wind outside the car was warm, so I stuck my head out. When we got to the lake, He didn't put my leash on like He usually does, which was strange because He told me one time, "You have to wear the leash, Bucko, so you'll always be close to me." He said it was okay though, so I got out of the car without my leash and stood close to him anyways because I felt safer, and otherwise He'd say, "No! Bad, Bucko, come!" I know I'm not bad, and I think He knows that too because He never sounds angry when He says I'm bad. He grabbed my ball off the car-seat and I ran fast ahead into the water.

He threw the ball far out into the lake for me like He always did, but He was quiet this time, which was not like He always was. All the other times we went to the lake He laughed and yelled out, "Good boy, Bucko, swim fast," because I'm a fast swimmer and He likes that about me. On that day He didn't laugh; He said, "Good boy," but not "swim fast." I didn't mind though, because He still thought I was a good boy, which I was, because I swam fast even though He didn't tell me to because I know it makes him happy. He threw the ball for forty-one minutes instead of forty-five, but I was okay with that because I swam extra fast that day and I was tired. When I got out of the water I sat straight up like I always did, dropped the ball in his paw, and waited for my towel. I like the towel because He always squeezes my whole body all at once and I bark, then He laughs because my bark makes him laugh, but I don't know what's funny. So I barked again when He put the towel on me, and He laughed, but this time it was quieter, like He was remembering a different bark that used to make him laugh. I wagged my tail anyway because I like it when He laughs.

The second day before He left, He put even more things in bags, which made me nervous, so I sat and chewed a bone because I wanted to be there if He needed my help like the day before. Also, He said we'd go on a walk if I waited and was a good boy, so that's what I did because I like walks. I watched him for thirty-four minutes until He suddenly stopped putting things in bags. He stood still for thirteen seconds, staring at something He was holding in his paws, like I do when I find a new smell. He came and knelt down to me, holding a small collar and smiling. It was strange because He didn't smell like He was smiling, because He actually smelled like He was scared, so I kept chewing on my bone. He placed the collar lightly on my nose, which made it tickle, and said, "Remember this, boy? It's your first collar from when you were a puppy. You were so little though, you probably don't remember." He scratched my ear for three seconds, which He knows I also like, plucked the collar from my nose, and put it into a bag. I do remember the collar from when I was a puppy, because I wasn't a puppy that long ago. I also remember the collar because He ruffled my neck for the first time after He put it on me, and I liked it right away.

We walked our usual path like we always did so I could say hi to other dogs, like Bento and Ratchet and Moxie, and squirrels, and so He could say hi to Mrs. Ellis. Mrs. Ellis lives close to us, and smells like cats which makes me want to pace and groan, but I have my leash on so I stay close. She also ruffles my neck, though differently than He does it, but I sit up straight anyway.

She said to Him, "I can't believe you're going in just two days! Did you know I changed your diapers when you were just a baby?" I didn't know what that meant, but He laughed and I perked my ears, and He said, "Yeah," but He stopped talking and played with his paws for two seconds and looked down at the ground. "It's hard to believe." I suddenly felt jealous because Mrs. Ellis had known him for longer, because I'd only known him for three years, and eight months, and fourteen days, but He didn't take her for walks so I stopped feeling jealous. They talked a little longer about something called the East Coast and "dog days," and then she hugged him. I didn't know what the East Coast or "dog days" were then, but He was happy while they talked, so I was happy. He said goodbye to Mrs. Ellis and finished our walk in silence.

The day before He left is the day He was sad, and so I was sad too. I went to his room so I could help him put things in bags, but when I got to his room, He was sitting on his bed and all the bags were closed up and on the floor. I guess He didn't want my help that day, but I sat straight up in front of him anyway. He wasn't smiling, or laughing, or ruffling my neck, or calling me a good boy. He sat staring at the bags for three minutes before He took a deep breath in and let it out slowly, which He only does when He's sad, so I put my chin on his leg because it usually makes him smile when He's sad. Instead of smiling, He put his face in my neck and held onto my paw with both of his paws, and then He started shaking and the fur on my neck got damp. He kept his head buried in my neck for two minutes before He looked at me again. His eyes were puffy and wet, and He looked at me differently than usual. I got nervous so I looked at the bags, but there were too many, so I closed my eyes. He took another deep breath in and let it out slowly. I did the same. Even though his paw was still wrapped around mine, I felt scared. They don't think we get scared very much, but we do.

We sat for six more minutes before Mom came in, slowly, with her head down, like I do after I eat out of the trash. They started to talk, and I don't always understand everything they say because they speak faster than I can swim, but I listen anyways because his voice makes me less scared. They don't think we listen, but we do. I heard Mom say, "Bucko will still be here, I won't let anything happen to him." I didn't understand, because I'm always here, and He's the one who goes places. He said back to her, "I know, but it's going to be different. He's always been there when I needed him. It's going to be hard not seeing him every day." I nudged my nose closer to him to tell him that I'm not going anywhere. This was a sad day. They don't think we know when it's a sad day, but we do. He put his head back into my neck and started shaking again.

He left the next day, and I barely felt like moving. I saw him in the doorway holding two bags, and smiling He said, "Come here Bucko!" He was smiling, but He didn't sound or smell like He was smiling. I got up anyway and followed, and I moved my tail just a little, even though I didn't feel like it, because He's my best friend and I wanted him to know that I was still His best friend. He set the bags down in front of the door, and He told me to sit, so I sat. Mom was standing just outside and her eyes were puffy and wet just like His were yesterday, so I felt scared again. He knelt down beside me and He told me, "Bucko, I'm going to be gone for a little while. I'm not going away forever, but I'm not going to be right back either." Instead of grabbing my paw, He wrapped his arms around my neck and buried his face below my ear, which meant that He was scared because He always puts his head above my ear when He's not scared, and I saw Mom turn away over his head. After eighty-five seconds He let go of my neck and took my paw in his paw. "Bucko, I need you to watch the house and take care of Mom, okay?" He looked me in the eyes and He tried to smile, but I know when He's really smiling and when He's pretending. They think we don't know, but we do. He sat up straight, expecting me to do the same like I always did. I felt too sad to sit up, so I dropped His paw for the first time and went to lie down in the corner. He stared at me for seventeen seconds, got up, picked up the bags, took one final deep breath and said, "I love you, Bucko." Then they walked out the door.

That was one year, and five months, and thirteen days ago. He said He wouldn't be gone forever, but each day felt like forever was getting closer and closer, because we know what forever is. Mom went to see him on the East Coast, but they said I had to stay here to watch the house. I feel sadder each time they don't let me come with them, but I continue to watch the house because that's what He told me to do, and I want Him to know that I am still His best friend.

Today has been a little different, though. Mom has been smiling all day, and she tells me that she is going to see him again soon. She doesn't tell me to watch the house when she leaves, but I will anyway because it makes Him happy. I curl up in my corner and go to sleep because sometimes I dream about Him. They don't know that we dream about them, but we do. They also don't know that sometimes we don't want to stop dreaming.

I don't know how long it's been when I hear the door open, but I hear his voice and I think I'm still dreaming. I hear him call, "Bucko! I'm back boy," but I've had this dream before, so I take a deep breath like He did one year, and five months, and thirteen days ago, and keep my eyes closed. I hear footsteps, and suddenly my back starts ruffling very hard, so I snap my eyes open. I see a man smiling down at me, and His face looks familiar, but I don't recognize Him at first. When I meet His gaze He begins to laugh and then I know it's Him, and I get up faster than I've ever even swam before and knock him to the ground.

I am so happy, happier than I've ever been because after one year, and five months, and thirteen days He is finally back! But I am also so mad at Him for leaving, madder than I've ever been, so I bite down on His arm like a bone, but He only laughs harder and pulls me into his arms, paws grasped tight around my neck. He ruffles my neck again in the way that only He does it, not like Mrs. Ellis, or even Mom, and I am no longer mad, but I keep biting down on His arm because I don't know what else to do. After two minutes of wrestling around on the ground we are both out of breath and He gets up on one knee. He looks at my eyes and I feel like He has never left, that He's only been gone a few days. I eagerly sit up straight and slap my paw down hard on His leg. He laughs, takes my paw in His paw, sits up straight, I wag my tail, and one year, and five months, and thirteen days after the horrible "dog days," he says, "Good boy, Bucko."

He still goes away for a long time after He comes home for a short time. After He left again for a long time, I was confused and scared because I thought He was staying for good again, but He wasn't. They think we understand, but we don't. I don't know where He goes, or what He does, or what the East Coast is, or why the final days of summer are called the "dog days," but I do know now that He always comes back. Sometimes I want to chew on my bones or his ball glove, so I don't always come right when He calls me, when He's home. I see Him watching me when I chew on bones. They don't think we watch them, but we do. He looks confused, like He doesn't understand how I could be happy without him, chewing on my bones or his ball glove. But when I'm done chewing I always go over to him and sit up straight, and slap my paw on his leg, and wag my tail, and He always laughs and ruffles my neck.

I think that when He leaves for a long time, He goes to chew on His own bones, or something that humans do that's like chewing on bones, because I've never seen Him actually chew on a bone. I'll watch Him leave and wonder how He could be happy without me, chewing on His own bones.

But when He's done chewing He always comes home, like He used to before the "dog days," and ruffles my neck, and wrestles with me, and lets me chew on his arm like a bone, and I know He's so happy, like when we're at the lake. I may not know why He always leaves, but I always keep track of how long He's gone, because He's my best friend, and I want Him to always know that I will be here, always waiting, even when Mom is gone and I'm alone, chewing on my bones. They don't know that we always wait. They don't know that I can wait for however long He's gone, even if He never comes back. But I know He always comes back. They don't think that we know.

     But we do.

The Music Lesson

Alec Clayton

As first dates go, this one was outstanding. She had the biggest eyes he had ever seen, and deep dimples. He loved dimples. The meal was enjoyable and not too heavy. He was confident that he came across as witty and sincere. When he took her home she invited him up for a drink. They sat side-by-side on the couch, she with her feet tucked yoga style. At last he worked up the nerve to kiss her and she responded, if not passionately at least firmly. Deciding not to pussyfoot around, he reached between her legs.

"No," she said, pulling his hand away.

"No? Not gonna happen?"

"Nope. Sorry. Not gonna happen."

She didn't seem upset, just determined in her rejection, and that was all right. At least he knew. That was always the question about a date. Is it going to lead to sex sooner or later, or just friendship or fall flat and die? She untucked her legs and sat forward on the edge of the couch with her knees together.

He said, "Let's get to know each other better. Music always says a lot about a person, what you like or don't like and why. So what's your favorite song?"

She shot him a quizzical look.

He said, "I know. Nobody has just one favorite. But think about it for a moment. If you can think of one song that really, really gets to you, what would it be?"

After a moment she said, "Imagine by John Lennon.

She sang a verse.

Imagine there's no countries

It isn't hard to do

Nothing to kill or die for

And no religion too . . ."

"There you go," he said. "Wow! That tells me a lot about you. Your thoughts, your beliefs, your heart."

"You're right. Yeah it does."

"We could be soul mates. Really."

She resettled on the couch, her legs tucked under her again. Her already big eyes opened wider. She even put her hand familiarly if platonically on his leg in a gesture that said we can be good buddies now, buddy.

She said, "You know what else gets to me every time? You're gonna laugh." She paused for a moment as if embarrassed, and then said, The Star Spangled Banner."

He didn't laugh.

She said, "I'm not nationalistic. I'm not an uber-patriot or anything, but there's something about that song that's soul stirring. It gets to me every time."

He said, "Did you know that it was originally quite different? I saw something on TV about that. As originally written it was played at a faster tempo and more like a march."

"Yeah, I know. I saw that too."

"They played a bit of the original, and I didn't like it."

"Me neither, but I guess it's just a matter of what we're used to."

They were quiet for a moment, and then she said, "OK, now it's your turn. What song grips your soul every time you hear it?"

It didn't take him long to think about it. "Bring Him Home from Les Miz."

"Whew! Oh God yes. Oh, that . . . that tells me so much . . . That, that's the song that does it for you. Hey, you know what? You know where I told you not to put your hand? Well why don't you put it back down there? I think maybe it's gonna happen after all."

There was little more to say until . . . after a while he said, "I love music."

Eleventh Hour Brother

An Arthur Beautyman Mystery

Erik Hanberg

The state of South Dakota would have executed an innocent man if Arthur Beautyman hadn't cleared the man's name while sitting on a sofa three hundred miles away.

Deidre Kirkpatrick, a wealthy 96-year-old recluse, had been found with a charred cantaloupe-sized hole in her chest. The list of suspects was short. Her only visitors anymore were her two sons and the medics who were regularly summoned by her medical alert pendant.

When the police located her son Ethan, they discovered his left hand was blackened and missing two fingers. A result of the same explosion that had killed his mother? Had Ethan rigged a miniature explosive device to kill her, accidentally losing two fingers in the process?

Unusual, to be sure, but the facts were clear to the South Dakota District Attorney. He pressed for the death penalty against Ethan and the jury agreed. Now, after years of failed appeals and protests of innocence, Ethan Kirkpatrick had just one hour left before his midnight execution.

"What a bizarre story," Ruth Beautyman murmured, watching the news coverage from her home in Minneapolis.

Ruth's adult son, Arthur, had only been half-listening, his attention mostly on his iPad. He would have preferred to be downstairs in her basement, chatting online with fellow "computer enthusiasts" (A.K.A—"hackers"). But after he was fired from the L.A. County Sheriff's Department for a massively public embarrassment, he had no badge, a terrible reputation, and nowhere else to turn than his mother's basement in Minnesota.

The least he could do was watch TV with her now and then.

So here he was. Participating.

Ruth shook her head. "Bombed his own mother to get his hands on her fortune a few years early."

"Just one hand now," Beautyman joked.

Ruth laughed but shushed him for being crude.

The TV showed a clip of Ethan in court, and Beautyman jumped. "Hey! I know that guy!"

"You do?" Ruth was shocked.

"We had a drink together once. At a technology conference in Vegas maybe six

years ago. He'd started a company that was pioneering some kind of keyless entry into your car and front door… or something. It didn't seem to be going well."

"The news said he went bankrupt. Penniless. Then a few months later… this."

When Beautyman had met him, Ethan had seemed like a fool—a half-baked idea in his head and too much money to throw at it. But a killer? Of his own mother? He'd told Beautyman that his mother and brother had been his first—and only— investors and he didn't seem to bear any ill will toward them.

Yet the evidence was overwhelmingly against him. Even Ethan's own version was damning: He admitted that no one else was in the room, for one. His mother's chest had simply exploded in front of him, he testified. His hand was injured. He got scared and ran.

It was possibly the worst alibi Beautyman had ever heard.

Nevertheless, he felt a tingling sensation on his neck, something he'd grown to trust over the years.

He opened his iPad and searched the web. The more he learned about Ethan and his keyless entry company, the more he saw a possible alternate version of events.

"Who inherited Deidre's fortune?" Beautyman asked his mother.

"It was supposed to be split evenly between Ethan and his brother Wesley. But once Ethan was convicted…"

"… his brother got everything," Beautyman concluded. He searched for Wesley Kirkpatrick.

Retired military. No obvious explosives experience that Beautyman could find, but that wasn't definitive. A military officer was more likely to know how to build a small bomb than the hapless man Beautyman had met in Las Vegas.

Beautyman was almost certain he could paint the overall picture. Wesley had invested in Ethan's company and had probably lost a good deal of money, just as Ethan had. Broke, he killed his mother, framed Ethan for it, and inherited the entire fortune himself.

Beautyman could almost prove it.

But almost wasn't enough.

He checked the time.

11:18.

Excusing himself to the basement, Beautyman went to his computer in the basement and quickly began a search of the deep web. Cell phone numbers were notoriously hard to find, but this is what he was good at. Using hacker forums and public web listings, he found the two numbers he needed within twenty minutes.

11:36.

He pulled an old pre-paid cell phone from one of his many bins of gadgets and began charging it. As soon as it illuminated, he sent his message—now untraceable back to himself:

Wesley, I know you killed your mother.

The reply was instantaneous:

WHO IS THIS?

Beautyman ignored it and continued:

Ethan's company sold RFID transmitters that were surgically inserted into people's palms, allowing them to unlock doors without a key.

He tested it on himself first, putting a chip in his own palm. He never had it removed.

You created a bomb and placed it on Deidre's chest. Probably camouflaged as her medical alert pendant.

Its trigger was proximity to the RFID tag in Ethan's palm. When he got within range—boom.

You almost got away with it.

Almost.

I'm texting you the private cell phone number for the governor of South Dakota.

Call him NOW. Confess.

If you call, you might get off with just a life sentence. If you don't, I will turn you in and you will be exactly where your brother is right now. With no one to save you at the 11th hour.

I will give you 10 minutes to make the call before I call myself.

Beautyman took the phone upstairs and sat down again, intent on the newscast.

11:48.

11:49.

11:50.

11:51.

A breaking news alert! The governor of South Dakota had stayed the execution!

Ruth gaped at her son. He just smiled.

Together they watched the governor announce the pardon, and Beautyman thought that he'd never been so happy to sit and watch the news with his mother.

Authors Featured in
Creative Colloquy Volume One
(In Alphabetical Order)

Titus Burley

Burley is a writer of maudlin poetry, navel gazing bloggery, stinging satire, and riveting short and long form fiction. He also authors memorable private messages to friends on social networks. His blog is viewable at titusburley.wordpress.com.

Perry Buto

Buto is a writer and an avid knitter originally from Honolulu, Hawai'i. Currently, she is completing her senior year at the University of Puget Sound, where she is majoring in Creative Writing and minoring in Japanese. Perry has previously been published in the University of Puget Sound's literary & arts magazine, *Crosscurrents*, and has a blog dedicated to showcasing easy knitting projects to the public, *Simple Knits*, which can be found at aknitaday.blogspot.com.

Jack Cameron

Cameron is native Tacoma writer. His work can be found at TacomaStories.com and JackCameron.com. He also wrote the self-destruct guide, *Ruin Your Life*. His first novel is *A Better Lie*.

Christian Carvajal

Carvajal is the author of *Lightfall*, a 2009 novel released by Fear Nought Publishing, and he's currently shopping a new novel with the working title *Mr. Klein's Wild Ride*. His work has been published in Cinefex and Literary Cavalcade, and he's a regular theatre critic and feature writer for the *Weekly Volcano*."Carv's Thinky Blog" is at ChristianCarvajal.com, along with purchase information for his nonfiction e-book, *Re-reading the Bible: Agnostic Insights Into Genesis, the Gospels, and Revelation*.

Alec Clayton

Clayton is a self-published novelist and feature writer. His work includes six novels and a book about art with the latest novel is due out this summer. Clayton writes a theater review column for *The News Tribune* and an art review column for the *Weekly Volcano*. He resides in Olympia with wife, Gabi. Together they founded and run Mud Flat Press (www.mudflatpress.com).

Ross Dohrmann

travel and

Dohrmann is originally from the San Francisco Bay Area. He moved to Tacoma in 2010 to attend UPS, from which he graduated in 2014. Aside from reading, writing and playing guitar, Dohrmann loves to do "outdoorsy" stuff like hiking, running, and kayaking.

Jonny Eberle

Eberle is a Southwest transplant living in Tacoma. He has a Bachelor's degree in Journalism and Political Science from Northern Arizona University and was the opinion editor of his campus newspaper, where a disgruntled reader once threatened to throw him off a roof. He blogs at www.jweberle.com.

Dawn Ellis

Ellis is a 31-year English teaching veteran of students, grades 6-12, in the small, rural community of Orting. As a native of the Tacoma and Gig Harbor areas, she attended Jefferson Elementary, Mason Middle School, and Peninsula High School. Living most of my life in "beach cabins," Ellis has a great appreciation for the Puget Sound. She has two children in the Air Force, one a pilot, the other in Global Intelligence. Want to play golf? She is a golf addict.

David Fewster

Fewster's journalism essays, fiction and poetry have appeared in numerous publications including *LA Weekly, the Seattle Sunday Times, the Stranger, Seattle Weekly, Writer's Digest*, and the anthologies *Seattle Poems by Seattle Poets* (Poetry Around Press, 1992), *Revival: Spoken Word from Lollapalooza 94* (Manic D Press, 1995), *Thus Spake the Corpse: An Exquisite Corpse Reader Vol. 2* (Black Sparrow Press, 2000) and *20/20: Tacoma in Images and Verse* (Peter Serko, 2010). He was a recipient of a 2003/2004 Tacoma Artists' Initiative Project grant for his book *"Diary of a Homeless Alcoholic Suicidal Maniac & other picture postcards."*

Lory French

Born in Charleston, SC, French decided at 8 years of age to move to the Puget Sound region. Now a blogger and home educator, French resides in Tacoma with her husband, three children, ten chickens, three dogs and two fish.

Michael Haeflinger

Haeflinger is a native Midwesterner who has recently moved to Tacoma from Philadelphia. His chapbook, *Love Poem for the Everyday* was published by Dog On a Chain Press in 2011 and his newest chapbook collection, *The Days Before*, will appear in Fall 2014. In addition to writing poetry, he also works on mixed media collages. Check out his work on the web at www.michaelhaeflinger.com

Erik Hanberg

Hanberg is the author of three mysteries, a science fiction adventure novel, and guidebooks for small nonprofits. He runs the boutique marketing firm Side x Side Creative with his wife Mary, and is an elected commissioner on the Metro Parks Board of Tacoma. Find him at erikhanberg.com or on Twitter at @erikhanberg.

Josh Kilen

Kilen is a Tacoma-based publishing writer with more than 15 books on topics ranging from Children's Fantasy to Marketing for Artists. Go to joshkilen.com to find out more.

L. Lisa Lawrence

Lawrence is an award winning writer whose work is featured in every issue of *South Sound Magazine*. She also contributed three sections to the *South Sound User Guide* and her work has appeared in many international publications. Her work encompasses: technical, spiritual, political, garden, home, cooking, urban farming, sustainability, inspirational, humor and travel writing as well as web page authoring, social media and blogging. See more of her work at wildcelticrose.net

Tiffany Aldrich MacBain	MacBain teaches American and Native American literature at the University of Puget Sound. She is writing a collection of essays on her experiences with motherhood and personhood in Tacoma and beyond. She has recently started a blog: http://amerethread.blogspot.com/
Lorna McGinnis	McGinnis is a student at the University of Puget Sound, in Tacoma, with an English major and a Spanish minor. She practices many different types of creative writing including screenwriting, short stories, and poetry. In her free time she enjoys Agatha Christie and martial arts
Ellen Miffitt	Growing up in rural Connecticut kept Miffitt close to the earth and nature. As a visual artist and as an art instructor, she has over forty years of experience. Miffitt's art may be seen at The Gallery, Bainbridge Arts and Crafts on Bainbridge Island WA, Gallery Boom in Tumwater WA and exhibits regionally and nationally.
Justin Racine	Racine came to the Colloquy's open mic as a guest. A young man of 21, though he has moved to Wausau, Wisconsin for college, he hopes to come back once he graduates. His other works of poetry is online at deviantart.com/hermitassasin. Although not a social person, he doesn't mind enjoying new company and comments.
Dan Rahe	Rahe has lived in Tacoma since 2007 and is active in various community volunteering endeavors. Until recently, he served as Editor in Chief of *Post Defiance*, an online publication covering Tacoma arts and culture.
The Red Hat Man	The Red Hat Man writes and creates in Tacoma Washington. He uses poetry to express his observations anyone can interpret into their own lives. To find out who The Red Hat Man is and/or share your thoughts with him, email; Random68@mail.com.
Nicholas Stillman	Stillman is a senior at the University of Washington Tacoma, where he studies writing and global engagement. He is also the former fiction editor of UWT's *Tahoma West* literary arts magazine. He has two cats, one wife, and a vintage Royal typewriter that he thought he was going to use for writing one day. They all live together in small brick building on Hilltop where they can be found making Mexican food and drinking beer (the people can, not the cats and typewriter).
Nick Stokes	Stokes has worked as a high school physics teacher, a wilderness ranger, an apple picker, a trail crew leader, a stable hand, a corn detassler, a tribology researcher, and is still a mule packer. For more information on his fictions, plays, and prose visit nickstokes.net. His novel *AFFAIR*, first serialized by *The Seattle Star*, is available at Amazon and elsewhere.

Melissa Thayer	Sin City native Thayer was born at a young age on a Sunday during a volcanic eruption and has been causing problems ever since. She writes fiction that touches upon the timeless truths of the human condition in poignant and thought-provoking ways (at least that's what someone either very nice or very well-paid said), and when not writing can be found generally poking fun at existence. Her debut novel *The Stories We Don't Tell* was published in 2014 through Booktrope.
Karen Harris Tully	Tully is in the process of querying agents for her debut novel, *Sunny from Afaar,* a YA sci-fi novel. "Janie's Got a Car" is her first attempt at a short story. She has a Bachelor's degree in Political Science and Economics from WWU, and lives in the small town of Raymond, WA with her amazingly supportive husband Mike and their beautiful son Gabe.
William Turbyfill	Turbyfill was born in Lickskillet, Alabama. He enjoys Doctor Who and the idea of Ben Affleck as Batman and he once met the Queen of England. He thinks she enjoyed it.

Michaela Eaves (Artist)	Eaves' childhood set up her adult life to be rich with a love of animals and nature, two themes present in her artwork. She pieces her professional life together with design work, fantasy and horror illustration, and traditional stylized painting. She is the illustrator and author of *42 Sketches* and is featured in the red deck of Tacoma playing cards. In her free time, she plays with her rescued Rottweilers and volunteers for non-profits.
Jackie Fender (Founder)	Fender has been a resident of Tacoma and surrounding areas since she was just a glimmer. She is self employed as a regular contributor to the *Weekly Volcano*, Assistant Producer of Duchess of Downtown Tours, Marketing Assistant for Puyallup Main Street and volunteer. She founded Creative Colloquy in February of 2014.
Joshua Swainston (Editor)	Swainston's short stories and flash fiction are printed in *Out of the Gutter, The Frist Line, Revolt Daily* as well as others. His self-published novel, *The Tacoma Pill Junkies*, was released in February of 2013 and can be found at tacomapilljunkies.com. He is currently the Editor-at-Large for *Creative Colloquy*.

Made in the USA
San Bernardino, CA
12 November 2014